Get Your Foot Out of Your Mouth

The Entrepreneur's Guide to Taking Action

Michelle Barr

Get Your Foot Out of Your Mouth: The Entrepreneur's Guide to Taking Action
Copyright © 2015 by Michelle Barr

ISBN 978-1-940170-71-8

Printed in USA

Dedication

To my husband, Roger, who has always supported me to go for my dreams; this is only the beginning!

To my amazing children who are out there in the world now creating the dream lives they desire and deserve; Craig, Hannah, and Haley, I love you so much!

For all those out there who have a life's calling they want to pursue as their work in the world, it's possible and it's doable! Borrow my belief until you have created your own.

Thank you to Suzanne Evans and Larry Winget for showing me the way and urging and encouraging me to stay in the game and move forward in the direction of my dreams and desires.

To my Father for being one of my first Entrepreneurial role models who never gave up and made his dreams come true, and for my Mother and Father both who have always taught me to live my life to its fullest, to never settle, to travel all over the world and do things I love. Thank you for buying me my first typewriter when I was 9.

It's time to stop talking and start walking in the direction of your dreams and desires.

How much time and energy have you spent talking about what you want to do? And what are you doing about it?

If you're being honest with yourself, it sounds like you need to get your foot out of your mouth and move your feet into Inspired Action, and Michelle Barr, Business Coach, Intuitive Strategist and Mindset Mentor is here to guide you.

Everyone around you is talking about what they're going to do, but, really, is anything actually happening?

Talk is cheap. It's what you do that counts.

The Entrepreneur's Guide to Taking Action is going to help you get your dream out of your head and into the world.

This isn't about just doing, doing, doing. This is about mastering the art of Taking Inspired Action.

Now, let's get those boots on the ground and get M.O.V.E.'ing!

<u>www.theentrepreneursguidetotakingaction.com</u>

"When we begin to dream big dreams, to set intentions and goals for ourselves, when we begin to strive for prosperity, abundance, health, wealth and success, everything that is not in alignment with that rises up to be healed or transformed. We must heal so that we can soar."

-- Michelle Barr

Table of Contents

Preface

People call me and email me every day telling me what they most want and why they don't and can't have it.

Too many people never take any action toward what they say they want most then wonder why they don't have it. This leads to one of two things: a lot of shame, blame, guilt, self-doubt, self-sabotage, and anger turned inward; or resentment, criticism, judgment, shame, blame, and anger turned outward toward those who have created what they want to be, do and have.

I spent a lot of years not having what I said I wanted most, and I had a lot of reasons why I didn't have it, couldn't have it, shouldn't have it, or just not now. Then, I made a decision to have it, right now. I took Action. I didn't just start running around doing, doing, doing, though. I cleared the mental and emotional clutter, I made a decision, I owned it 100%, I created a Vision of the life I wanted to live, and I took Inspired Action.

Now, I have the life I want to live and the business that supports and sustains it, and I am showing other Entrepreneurs how to do the same.

I believe that building your own business is the most intensive personal growth and development program you could ever enroll in. It's a Journey, and it will grow you like nothing else. At this point in my Journey, I would never go back. The payoffs are so worth it. There are just some things you are going to want to know.

To me, this is the ultimate Freedom, to create a Vision of the life you want to live and then create a business that allows you to live that life. I see so many people doing the opposite. They are living a life dictated by the work they are doing and the conditions created by it. They don't love what they are doing, and they don't even like their lives. Year after year, nothing changes. Year after year, they keep telling themselves, they are going to have what they most want and live the life they most want to live... some day.

If you are ready to be committed to living the life that you most want to live, I want you to know you can live that life now and at every season and stage.

I will show you how to build a business that supports and sustains the life you want to live. It's so possible and more doable than you believe it is.

People hire me every day to help them do what I have done and what I know how to guide and support you in doing. I have been where you are. I have lived it over and over again. For way too long.

Then the day came when I stopped talking about not having it and decided to have it instead.

Once you discover how to give yourself this Freedom, you will be able to do it every time you find yourself in a place where you identify that there is something you most want that you don't have.

This book is not for people who want to stay in jobs they don't like doing work they don't love. What I am going to share with you is for people who are ready to make a decision to get clear on what they most want and then take Action to create it for themselves.

I am asking you right here to Trust the Process.

The principles I share with you in this book are things I apply to building and growing my business and to living my life in all areas, as well. The focus here is for Creative, Intuitive, Inspired Entrepreneurs who have a Vision and know they aren't living it or who have lost touch with their Vision altogether. Maybe you don't think you are Creative or Intuitive, and you aren't feeling very Inspired right now? That's okay. This work will open you up to accessing more of yourself and bringing it out into the world.

This book and these principles will be especially embraced by Life Coaches, Business Coaches, Counselors, Teachers, Speakers and Authors, and Helpers and Healers of all kinds. I know this, because I have a proven track record of working with them.

We will start here.

Create a Vision. Create a Business. Create a Life.

Michelle Barr

Notes:

Chapter One: From Living By Default to Living By Design

"Default living comes as a result of operating from a reactive place and making decisions from an unbalanced 'fight or flight' state of emergency and stress all the time. We are allowing programmed thoughts, beliefs and scripts to navigate and guide our actions. We are letting the unconscious drive our bus. (This is a big part of the reason why using The Law of Attraction isn't as effective for us as we'd like it to be.)"

Sometimes it still amazes me what I have created here.

I mean, I really did it! After turning my life into an experiment for the Law of Attraction, I have completely shifted Living By Default into Living By Design.

I lived by default because I wasn't in control. Everyone else was. Others called the shots; I just followed along. My husband, parents, children, friends and co-workers controlled my emotions. My job controlled my work hours and paychecks. I submitted myself to the demands and expectations of others without regard to the effects it would have on me.

Despite the circumstances, I figured living by default was the norm. It was how life was meant to be – miserable and unfulfilling. *We can't all be happy all the time*, I thought. And, believe me, there are plenty of people who will gather around you and support THAT belief.

When I came to that place in 2003 where I was sick of everything in my life, I couldn't believe it. I had been here before. The first time, I had taken control of myself and my life, gone through an intense personal awakening, and had created a whole new life. Yet, a decade and a half later, here I was again.

I've rebooted my life from miserable circumstances – including an unhappy marriage and draining career – TWICE. The second time, it stuck!

The first time I was just intuitive and just awakened enough to pull myself out of my miserable circumstances and create a better life. The problem was, I didn't know what I was doing. I wasn't consciously creating. So I ended up creating some of what I wanted and a lot of what I didn't.

It wasn't until I committed myself to learning how to consciously create life on my terms that I transformed my life for the better with lasting results.

When all the buzz began about the Law of Attraction and I woke up a second time, I knew they were saying something that felt right. It was like I was being reminded of something I already knew. But I, like many others, struggled to use the Universal Principles put forth to me to transform my life for the better.

Something inside of me recognized I was standing at this place again, with some sort of do-over, a pop quiz from the Universe to do it differently this time. And this time, I finally learned how to master it.

I embarked on a journey that day that I may not have agreed to if I had known where it would take me. But, from where I stand now, I would do it all over again.

If you are one of those people who feel that "The Secret" and the whole Law of Attraction movement failed them, I get it. "The Secret" served a purpose of bringing this Ancient Wisdom and Universal Thought into the mass consciousness, but, in order to do that, it had to be watered down.

People watched the movies, read the books, listened to the audios over and over, joined groups to help them make it work, carried rose quartz in their purse, alongside their gratitude journal, updated daily with "5 Things I am Grateful for Today..." And, still, it just wasn't working.

After several weeks or even months of practice, many people failed to manifest what they most desired. They still didn't love their work. They still didn't have enough money. Their marriage was still on the rocks. Their spouse still threatened to leave. Their children refused to behave. Creditors and bill collectors continued to call.

Since they failed to get results, they figured the Law of Attraction was nothing more than feel-good "woo-woo hocus pocus." It might work for some, but for the most part, they decided it was for suckers, and they discarded the beliefs they had been holding onto like a lifeline, felt jilted, and resigned themselves to living their life as is, by default.

Still, something about this whole Law of Attraction thing was ringing true to me. I decided, what did I have to lose? I already was dissatisfied with my life. I was pretty miserable. So, I made that decision in the heat of an inspired moment to turn my life into an experiment for the Law of Attraction. I could not have known how it would completely transform not only my life but the life of my husband and children, and it would become not just my life but my life's work.

You see, the problem was and is *not* The Law of Attraction. The Law of Attraction works. In fact, it's infallible, and it's on 24 hours a day, 7 days a week, whether you believe in it or not. You just have to understand how to work with it.

The truth is, you can't get what you want by just thinking happy thoughts about it. You have to take Action. That is the real secret. It's the key to everything.

After all that, this is going to seem so simple, possibly too simple, but here is how it works. To make it even easier for you, as you are learning something new and putting it into practice, I have broken it down into a simple exercise with four simple steps. Take out a blank index card.

1. Set an intention of something you want to create. Write it down on a notecard.

Be very clear. Be very specific. The important thing is to stay with what you want without regard to how it could happen. Leave the how's to the Universe. This is an important Universal Law that will absolutely determine your results.

2. Come up with new actions you are willing to take to make this happen. Write them down on the other side of the note card.

   This is not about springing into action and just doing, doing, doing. This is about getting into a quiet, reflective place and connecting with what you want and writing it down. Then, become inspired, and write down actions you are inspired to take.

   Ask and it is given is a Universal Principle. It is found in every sacred text, and it is absolutely true. When you ask, the Universe always begins delivering to you what you are asking for. Most people just aren't prepared for how it actually shows up in comparison to how they expect it to show up. When you ask, begin immediately to watch for opportunities to show up. And remember this, they will not be logical, comfortable or convenient. They will stretch and grow you. If you didn't need to grow and stretch to receive them, you would already have them.

3. Follow through with at least one.

Get into inspired, aligned action right away. Take one action, then watch for feedback. Stay in action. Learn to Act, Assess, and Adjust. Course correct as needed. Just don't stop. The Universe will continue to give you feedback. Watch for breadcrumbs, and follow the breadcrumbs, even when, ESPECIALLY when they don't make sense. Just follow the breadcrumbs.

4. Make it happen! And watch the Universe go to work for you.

The Universe responds to true need. It does not play the when/then game. You always have to take the first step. Then it will rush in to support you. You are building a trust muscle here. Try this first with small things, less important things. Don't try this right away with things that trigger you emotionally. The easiest things to manifest are those which you have High Desire for and Low Resistance to.

Hang on to the card. Hang it up where you can see it. Track your progress on it. This works best when you can stay engaged but detached from the outcome. You can affirm and write on the card, "Thank you for this or something better." Leave the door open for something to show up that is better than what you are asking for. You can't even imagine the miracles the Universe can deliver to you! And, when it shows up, express gratitude, and tack the card up on your celebration board or tuck it into your gratitude journal, and go for the next one.

The key here is these things at first are things you do. They are new ways of thinking, new patterns of behavior, new ways of doing things. And, over time, they become more than things you do. They become a way of living, and a way of being.

Right before your eyes, your life will Transform.

Living this way has allowed me to create a Vision of the life I want to live and then create a business that supports and sustains that life, and it changes with me, it grows and evolves with me. It always supports me and my life first, and as I am supported, I am able to touch and impact many in the world.

Notes:

Chapter Two: My IOA Formula for Success

When you want something better, something more for yourself, your most important first step is to realize that it is up to you to create a better life, and then know that you can do that starting right now. In working with my private coaching clients, I find that positive changes and new results can begin to show up within the first 30 days, and by the end of 90 days of working consciously to create a better life, many things have come to them, and their lives truly are more satisfying, fulfilling, and joyful.

No matter what you want to do, no matter what you want to work on, no matter what area of your life you are ready to make changes in, the principles and processes for that are the same.

Everybody who teaches about success principles is talking to you about taking Action, and there's a reason why. It is the place where dreams become reality, where desires are made manifest, and taking Action is the only way to bring your Vision into your waking world.

Action is what manifests things for you on the third-dimensional plane, right here, so it shows up in your life. But you don't want to take just any Action, and you don't want to just be doing, doing, doing; you want to learn to receive Inspiration and then experience the power that comes with taking Inspired Action.

It is important to first develop your gifts, abilities, and skills in your life, and then to learn to use the IOA Formula for Success – Intention, Opportunity, Action. The IOA integrates these three action steps with the use of your Intuition, your Energy, and your Mindset. The result is Magic!

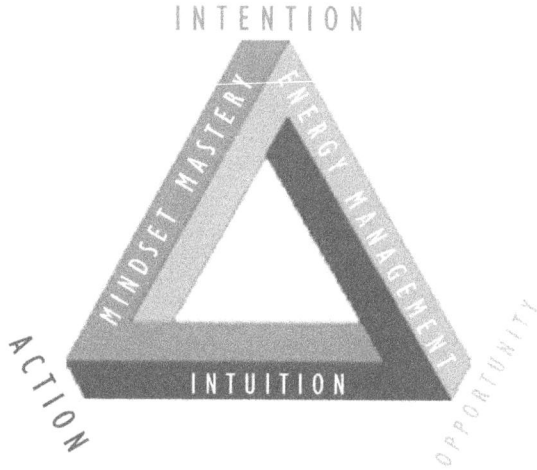

INTENTION

MINDSET MASTERY

ENERGY MANAGEMENT

ACTION

OPPORTUNITY

INTUITION

INTUITIVESUCCESSCOACH.COM

This allows you to take your dreams and Vision and live into them here and now so they actually show up in your physical world. You learn first to reconnect your personal and creative energy with your physical reality, and then you learn how to Master the Art of Taking Action. But remember, not just any Action. INSPIRED ACTION.

The best news is, you don't even have to ask yourself, well, is this right for me? Will this help me right now? Maybe, I'm not ready. I don't have all my ducks in a row. I made space for this in my life plan, but later. I'm setting the stage. I'm setting the table. STOP!

I am an expert at helping people get into Action, and I will tell you this – this will work for you whether you are a baby-stepper or a ledge-leaper. I work with both, and the results are the same. The reason it works is because it all works with your Energy.

You've got to get to the Action. The truth is, it takes third-dimensional Action to create third-dimensional results. It takes massive third-dimensional Action to create massive third-dimensional results. That means you have to come out of your head and come out of the ethers and make this thing happen for you in real time. It's so much better that way. Really.

Getting Unstuck From Your "Stuff"

My passion is to get people out into the world using their gifts. This is a place where you can really get stuck, because you are putting yourself out there, and asking for something in return. This is when all your programs, beliefs, patterns and habits related to your value and your worth start showing themselves. You are stuck, you are having a personal crisis, or you're getting in your own way, but you also have this Vision, you know you have been called to do something, and you're trying to step out and do it.

That is when mastering the art of taking Action really works. Because that is when you can get in touch with your "Why," connect in with your Vision, your Mission, your Dreams and your own personal Truth, and act from a place of Purpose.

The minute you hear that calling and you respond, as soon as you step out and step up, when you have big dreams and big visions, you set big goals and intentions, the minute you do that, everything inside of you that is not in alignment with that comes up. I call it "your stuff," and it's part of the process.

But what it feels like is, I'm not strong enough to do this now, I'm trying to do this thing and look what's getting in the way. The Universe, God, Source, my Guides, my Inner Guidance and my Higher Self don't want me to do this right now.

I am here to tell you, this is a big shift to make, and it makes all the difference. Your Higher Self, your trusted Source, whatever name you call that, wants for you whatever you want for yourself. If there's a desire within you calling it forth, it is possible, and it's part of why you are here.

So you have that Big Vision, and then your stuff comes up.

Realize that your stuff coming up means you actually are doing the work! It's working, and just beyond it is the gold, is the life, is the success, is the freedom and release that you're searching for.

Looking at it this way reframes it. You can avoid going into crisis when this happens by realizing it is part of the process. Now you can work with it; use it as a catalyst. It is a tool for your personal and spiritual growth and development, an integral part of the process.

You have a feeling-guidance system inside of you. So when you step up and say, "I am successful," "I'm a business person," when you step up and say "I am going to Be more, Have more, and Do more," you are saying, "Use me, I am ready to be used." That is a big message you are sending out to the Universe, and the

Universe will usually respond in a big way.

Intention

"When you have something showing up in your life, it always started with an intention. That's great, if you have been consciously creating, but not always so much if you have been unconsciously creating."

It all starts with Desire. You have a Desire, and you set an Intention. You are always setting intentions, either consciously or unconsciously, and you then see what you are asking for and what you believe and expect showing up all around you.

The first thing I do when a client comes to me with something they don't want showing up in their life is to go back to when this first started occurring and see what they were asking for, either consciously or unconsciously. Always, a starting point can be found that began bringing the energy of this into physical form.

The key is to become more and more conscious about setting Intentions, and get clear, centered, focused and grounded. The number one thing that people come to me with is Confusion. So, your first step is to transform your Confusion into Clarity.

Confusion is one of the things I most often see keeping people stuck. Whatever you are asking, the Universe is answering, so keeping yourself in a state of Confusion is always a choice. You can choose to stay in a confused state. I will tell you, if you're staying in a confused state for any length of time, you're choosing to do that, and it's serving you.

There is something you are refusing to see, or there is

something you are refusing to respond to. It's there. Go back and take honest inventory and figure out why you are needing to stay in this state. Then take steps to move into Clarity. When faced with Confusion, there is always something you can do to move out of it.

Take 100% responsibility to push through your Confusion. Recognize it as Resistance.

Wherever there is a need and a desire, there is also the ability to fulfill it. Now.

Opportunity

"There is always a way forward from wherever you now stand."

When you set an intention, you activate "Ask and it is given." Every sacred text has a version of this, and yet many no longer believe it's true. It's not that it's not happening every day, it's that you aren't understanding it, and so you can't see it and use it.

The moment you ask, it is always given. So, now, you become hyper-alert, and you watch for what shows up. What is going to show up is opportunity, and it's up to you to see it and step into it. And here's the thing – it's not always going to show up as you expect it to, and it's not going to be comfortable. It's going to stretch you.

Here's why. You are asking for something that you don't currently have. It's not in your environment, because you are not yet a match for it. But you have desire for it, so it's in your energy, and now you have to bring it into physical form. You have to change something within yourself so that it can show up outside of you. If you could already possess it, you would.

Don't get stuck here! A lot of people do. I urge you not to misread what is showing up first and think it's a sign you aren't supposed to have this thing you desire, it's not time, or it's not right for you. Spirit wants for you what you want for yourself. Spirit created you to be a creator, and Spirit gave you free will. It's all here for you. You have to choose it. And you have to choose to be the person who can be it, do it, and have it.

As you seek to align yourself to this thing you desire, what shows up first feels and looks like a lot of crap. What you are seeing is everything that is currently not in alignment energetically with what you are wanting to bring in. It's telling you, you can have this thing you want, but here's what's going to have to go, here's what's going to have to be dealt with first.

What shows up next is Opportunity. Stay with it. Hold space for what you want. Focus your will, and stay the course. Here's another place where you might feel really frustrated. Self-doubt can kick in. I encourage you not to turn away from what you are bringing in, because then you get into start and stop energy, and what you desire stops moving toward you.

When that Opportunity shows up, you want to meet it head on. Step up and Take Action. That is when you see the results, and what you desire begins to show up in your world.

Action

"Make A Decision. It all starts right here. As soon as you do, you will set things in motion, and the Universe will conspire on your behalf. You have to take the first step. Every time."

Right after I created the body of work I call *Master the Art of Taking Action*, I had the opportunity to speak with Janet Switzer, Business Coach to Jack Canfield and many other well-known Transformational Leaders in the Human Potential Movement. As I was pitching her this work I was developing at the time, she said, "I see what you do. Your message to people is, 'Get over your garbage and take action!'" Well? Yes!

When I talk about my work, I talk about how to Master the Art of Taking Action so you can Get Moving in the Direction of Your Dreams and Desires and Create A Better Life Now! In all truth, how I got from where I was to where I am now was by learning how to, indeed, get over my garbage, and then I had to learn how to take action in an empowered and intuitive way that best serves me. I want the same for you, and I want it Now! Do you?

I see people like you. They show up as my clients and students, beginning to make new discoveries about themselves and their world and creating some powerful shifts in their thoughts and feelings and beliefs. Yet, they are still stuck, right at the point where it's time to take action. Can you relate?

As you clear away more and more of the mental and emotional clutter that can overtake your life and block you from your connection to your inspiration, you will discover, as I did, that you can create a better life now. Get over your garbage. Get over the constant beating up and second-guessing and sabotaging yourself. Get over feeling not enough.

You are here, now, and who you are is enough for someone. Your journey is important, and it can have an impact on others only when you are willing to share it. And here's the best part –

sharing it is what brings you the most reward - mentally, physically, emotionally, spiritually, and financially!

These are all a part of the process to Master the Art of Taking Action. This is what I work on with my clients and students as I continue to work on this in my own life. It has been life-changing and game-changing for me, and it absolutely can be for you, too. My life now is unrecognizable from the life I was living just 7 years ago and even 5 years ago.

My Coach's Request To You: If you are ready to Create A Better Life Now, make a Decision to do so. Next, set a Conscious Intention based on something you Desire. Immediately, begin watching for an Opportunity to show up, and, when it does, Take Action.

Notes:

Chapter Three: Why Am I Creating What I Don't Want?

Let's Start at the Very Beginning!

I'm going to take a page out of Julie Andrews' book. "Let's start at the very beginning. A very good place to start. When you read, you begin with ABC. When you sing, you begin with Do Re Mi..."

... When you manifest, you begin with IOA!

I want to make this really simple, so you can get started being the Conscious Creator of your own life.

So, start right now being very aware, very conscious of what is showing up in your life that you don't want and what is not showing up in your life that you do want.

When you have something showing up in your life, it always started with an intention. That's great, if you have been consciously creating, but not always so much if you have been unconsciously creating.

The first thing I do when a client comes to me with something they don't want showing up in their life is to go back to when this first started occurring and see what they were asking for, either consciously or unconsciously. Always, a starting point can be found that began bringing the energy of this into physical form.

You don't have to wait until the first day of a new year or the first day of a new month to move into the energy of new beginnings. Right now, right here, we're starting fresh, turning the page. Let's move forward right now into a positive process that will bring you the results you desire.

Here's something you can do that will show you very quickly what's up in your world and help you to create a better life now.

Forget New Year's resolutions. We all know they don't work. And it's no wonder why, when you look at the energy they are created from. You are connecting emotionally with things you are fighting in your life, and you are stating what you are going to STOP doing and what you are going to START doing. You are focusing on your bad habits, unhealthy patterns and toxic relationships and environments and giving them power by focusing on them. Besides, the mass consciousness has pretty much created an energy around "new year's resolutions" that we associate them with something that you are going to say and not follow through with and something that doesn't work. It doesn't feel good.

Instead, set an Intention. Start with one. It's best not to start with something you know you have a lot of negative emotional charge to and that you have a lot of resistance with. You will get to those once you've built some belief in this process and in yourself.

Take a moment to really connect in with your intention. This is the part where you activate "Ask and it is given." Every sacred text has a version of this, and yet many no longer believe it's true. It's not that it's not happening every day, it's that you aren't understanding it, and so you can't see it and use it.

The moment you ask, it is always given. So now you become hyper-alert, and you watch for what shows up. What is going to show up is opportunity, and it's up to you to see it and step into it. And here's the thing – it's not always going to show up as you expect it to, and it's not going to be comfortable. It's going to stretch you.

Here's why. You are asking for something that you don't currently have. It's not in your environment, because you are not yet a match for it. But you have desire for it, so it's in your energy, and now you have to bring it into physical form. So, you have to change something within yourself so that it can show up outside of you. If you could already possess it, you would.

Don't get stuck here! A lot of people do. They misread what is showing up first, and they think it's a sign they aren't supposed to have this thing they desire, it's not time, or it's not right for them. Spirit wants for you what you want for yourself. Spirit created us to be creators, and Spirit gave us free will. It's all here for us. We have to choose it. And we have to choose to be the person who can be it, do it and have it.

As you seek to align yourself to this thing you desire, what shows up first feels and looks like a lot of crap. What you are seeing is everything that is currently not in alignment energetically with what you are wanting to bring in. It's telling you, you can have this thing you want, but here's what's going to have to go, here's what's going to have to be dealt with first.

What shows up next is opportunity. Stay with it. Hold space for what you want. You have to focus your will here and stay the course. Here's another place where people get frustrated. Self-doubt kicks in. And they turn away from what they are bringing in, and it stops moving toward them.

When that opportunity shows up, you have to meet it head on. You have to step up and take action. And that is when you see the results, and what you desire begins to show up in your world.

Intention => Opportunity => Action

"When you know the notes to sing, you can sing most anything!"

Give it a try, and let me know what shows up for you! www.facebook.com/michellebbarr

Why Am I Creating What I Don't Want?

Think about it. That's a very different question than, *Why Am I Not Creating What I Want?* For really, there's no "not creating" about it. You are the Creator of your entire life, of your entire experience. Things don't happen *to* us, they happen *through* us.

I am intuitive and empathic and always have been, though for a very long time I didn't have a conscious awareness of this. Because of that, I have always been able to create things I wanted, AND I spent a lot of years creating a lot of what I didn't want, as well.

The Universe doesn't listen to your words and obey them. The Universe responds to your vibration, to what you are sending out through your thoughts which create feelings, and it is your feelings that are magnetic and attract to you a match to what you are sending out.

Imagine that you are sending out to the Universe a strong desire for the love of your life. You want it. You know you want it. You are sending this desire out into the Universe. Chances are, because you have such strong desire, you also have some resistance to your desire because of your attachment to it, your limiting beliefs, your bad habits and unhealthy patterns, and your toxic emotions. As you are sending out to the Universe your desire for the love of your life – you can feel it, you can see it, you have made your list about all the qualities you want it to show up with – you have to be aware of what else is going out in your request. Energetically.

Things that might get into the mix could include, "I've been hurt before. I am afraid to get hurt again," or, "I think I'm ready to open my heart and my life to someone else, but I'm not sure I'm ready. Am I really ready?" Unworthiness could be getting broadcast out in your request, along with not good enough, not enough, or fear, doubt, and guilt. The possibilities are endless, and most often we are unconscious of them, and yet they hold so much power in our creating.

Have you made room for your creation to show up – really, really made room? The Universe responds to a true vacuum and comes in to answer true need. If you are holding on to things and people that no longer serve you waiting for this new creation of your dreams to show up, it won't.

When it comes to creating, we operate on a continuum of conscious and unconscious creation, and at any given time we can be creating from anywhere along that continuum. If you picture yourself on this continuum with 0% to 100%, from unconscious creating to conscious creating, it is beneficial for you to increase your awareness of the energetic dynamic at play here. How much of the time are you creating unconsciously? This results in a lot of mis-creating and a lot of what you don't want showing up in the process. Now, how much of the time are you consciously creating, showing up as a Co-Creative partner with the Universe? THIS results in much more creating what you DO want.

Things happen through us. Our perspective deeply colors our world. The way we are looking at something and our awareness of the governing principles that we choose to adopt as our reality heavily influence what shows up for us.

A good tool or technique can shift the energy, which will create a shift, often noticeable, in your life. Yet, without the mindset to support this shift, you will revert back to the energy you were previously holding. You will fall back into the familiar patterns that you are comfortable with.

Today, I am going to share with you a series of principles that govern my life.

Notice as you read each one, which ones speak to you, which cause you to react, possibly in a negative or disbelieving way, and which ones are you neutral about at this time. If you do not agree, what do you currently believe instead? Just read each one and notice what comes up for you. Where this is a charge, there is gold to mine.

1. Energy flows where attention goes. What we resist persists. Pay close attention to what you are focusing on. What are you thinking about? What are you feeling? How much time are you spending focusing on what you want, and how much time are you spending focusing on what you don't want?

2. Everything counts. Everything matters. A choice point exists in every moment. Our life is shaped by the series of choices we make along the way. Become more conscious about the choices presented to you. Become more conscious of your ability to choose. This requires a shift in perspective from Victim to Creator. This requires taking completely responsibility for all of it.

3. Everything is Energy. You are an energetic being in energetic exchange with the Universe and everyone and everything in it. Learn about Your Own Universal Energy (Y.O.U. Energy) and how to use it to heal yourself and create your extraordinary life. Learn to work with this. Everything that shows up in your life is there for a reason. You can learn to interpret this, recognize it, heal and clear it, and create life YOUR way.

4. When we begin to dream big dreams, to set intentions and goals for ourselves, when we begin to strive for a more extraordinary life, everything that is not in alignment with that rises up to be healed or transformed. I call that, "Your stuff coming up." When you step into your intentions, dreams and goals, your "stuff" is going to come up. You can choose to heal and clear this so that you can move forward and step out of mediocrity into your most extraordinary expression and experience.

5. Learn to leave the How's to the Universe. Get to the essence of what you want. Dream big. See it, feel it, live it,

love it, be it. Don't waste your time asking, how? "How could THIS possibly happen for ME?" Don't let your logical mind take over and try to figure it all out. That will take you right into stories of limitation, scarcity and lack. The Universe can create miracles when we move out of the way.

6. Get out of your head and get out of your stories. We all have created stories we tell others and ourselves that define who we are and what our lives are about. These stories have power over us. They are highly charged with words and emotions. We can become trapped within our stories. Start recognizing what stories you are telling, then stop telling your stories.

7. The Law of Attraction is always on. It always exists whether you believe in it or not, whether you are actively working with it or not. It is not something you can spend time on here and there and get consistent results. A common misperception I see people making is that they set aside some time to meditate or journal or say their affirmations or attend a workshop, and then they step right back into living their life with their limiting beliefs, bad habits and unhealthy patterns, and toxic emotions driving their bus. And then they wonder why The Law of Attraction doesn't work.

8. Once you get into the flow, don't stop. Act, Access and Adjust. Keep going. So many people stop just short of acting. They hesitate, and then they miss the moment of the energy that has stepped in to meet them. You can learn to stay connected to Source/Creator energy and to receive inspired actions. Then it's still up to you to ACT.

9. Before the doing comes the being. This one is counterintuitive to a lot of people when they first start

working with it. Many people come for help, and they say, tell me what to do, and I'll do it… if you can guarantee that I'll get these results. They say that when they have something, they will do something that will allow them to be something. It doesn't work that way. You have to be the thing you want to be first. You have to do the things that people like that would do. And THEN you will have what people like that have. We call this the Be-Do-Have.

These Principles, once applied, become more than a way of doing things. They become a way of living, a way of being. You can get a free downloadable poster with the 9 Universal Guiding Principles at www.9UniversalGuidingPrinciples.com

Do the energetic work first. The more you learn to work with the energy of the creative process and the energy of YOU, the less action you are required to engage in. You begin to attract to you everything you need. Things begin to come together more easily and effortlessly in a way that you know is coming from the Universe.

Right now, in this moment, what is the most important thing you need to do?

Show up! This is key. Show up now and in every moment, a ready and willing partner with the Universe, excited to Co-Create. Show up, and trust that you already have everything you need.

Show up for yourself now.

I want you to be excited about your journey. You notice I didn't say get excited; I said BE excited! Your journey is now, always. You are on it, always have been. We need to stop holding the energy of "gonna" and "getting to" something.

Here's a secret! There is no failure; there are no mistakes. The more you begin to consciously create, the more you learn to Act, Assess and Adjust and the more you learn to make Course Corrections that save you a lot of time and energy and save you a lot of pain. Pain happens. Suffering is optional.

Helen Keller said, "Life is either a daring adventure or nothing."

Now is the perfect time to create your extraordinary life, to transcend self-imposed limits and break free from mis-creating unconsciously.

You have everything inside of you in this moment that you need.

There are no failures, no mistakes. You are on your path, always, and this is your journey. You get to choose what step you will take next.

Your WHOLE Life Is Waiting.

What are YOU waiting for?

I invite you to keep reading. I invite you to explore your own unlimited possibilities. I invite you to take inspired action, to step out of mediocrity and create your own extraordinary life!

Chapter Four: How to Start Strong to Get Into Action and Create What You Desire

"If your core is weak, nothing else can be strong."

By working first from the CORE, it will make you stronger mentally and emotionally and help you build a rock-solid foundation from which you can create everything else!

As the whole of you works together and is completely interrelated – body, mind and spirit – everything else relies on your core. It's your base, and your center of attraction.
Here's how to start strong and create what you desire.

C. Clarity

Confusion is one of the things I most often see keeping people stuck. Whenever you get stuck in Confusion, the first thing you want to do is create clarity. It can feel overwhelming, and you may feel like you're not ready or prepared to get clear. But that's because you are seeing and feeling your big picture, your big Vision. You only need to create clarity around this moment and your next step. When faced with Confusion, there is always something you can do to move out of Confusion.

Just start with, "What is one thing I need to know?" and when you are able to connect with that information, you can then take an action in that direction.

"I'm confused. I'm stuck." is an excuse. Confusion is a defense mechanism. It does not serve you. It creates a story, and allows you to live in that story, if you choose. It is a distraction, and it is ultimately avoidance.

Recognize it. Own it. Push through Resistance into Receptivity. Get started right now.

Here is a coaching tool I use with my clients, and it's yours. Now, here's the thing. I want you to use it. Use it once, right now or very soon, then hold onto it, add it to your toolbox, and use it often. This is just one of the powerfully practical and spiritually rich tools I use in my coaching program, and it works equally well for both your business and your life. Listen online or download it to go at http://instantteleseminar.com/?eventid=27572484.

O. Ownership

Getting clarity about the next thing you need to know leads way to an inspired action it is clear you must take next. Now, it's time to make a decision, and then take ownership of that decision. This is so important, because here's where a lot of people start to fall apart. The minute they get clarity and make the decision to take that next step, there is often a moment of euphoria followed by the ego fighting for its life. So, then you start second-guessing yourself, doubting yourself, playing back all the programs full of limited beliefs and toxic patterns, until there you are, spinning again.

It's takes a tremendous amount of creative energy to get yourself from here to where you want to be, especially those first few steps. So, you don't need anything draining your energy, and that's what those kinds of behaviors do.

As soon as you catch the clarity and make a decision, support yourself in that decision 100%. Sometimes, this takes practice, and, at first, you may only be able to support yourself 100% for a few minutes, a few hours, a day. Notice your own self-talk, and notice the stories you are telling others. It all counts. It all matters.

R. Receptivity

From this new energetic stance, you can begin to receive what you are asking for. Things will begin to show up for you in the physical when you start taking physical action.

Here is another sticking point for many people. You want to recognize that there is a Law of Giving and Receiving. Picture it like the infinity symbol. Some people have their giving blocked, and then there are those of you who are more likely to be reading this that have your receiving blocked.

You want to make sure you are open and allowing the good you are asking for. This is a big part of where doing the energetic work first brings you the best results.

E. Embodiment

Do you see what we are creating here? We get clear on what energetic stance to take and what next step we are going to commit to. Without that, none of the rest of this will bring you what you desire.

Once you are clear, you take ownership. You support yourself 100%. You hold onto your Vision and revisit it every day. It's your touchstone. All your energy is now being focused to support what you are wanting to create. Picture this as a hose with a strong concentrated spray rather than lots of trickles going off in all directions. Then you open to receive what you are asking for.

It is written in every sacred text, "Ask and it is given." And, it's true. You are always given the opportunity to create what you are asking for. It doesn't always show up in the way you expect it to. It's not always logical. And it's often not comfortable. Nevertheless, don't miss it when it shows up. The clearer you are, the more centered, grounded and focused you are, the quicker and easier it will all come together for you. Just like anything else, you want to execute it from a strong core.

The next step is to pull that focused energy right into you. Imagine it. Own it. Focus on it. Receive it. And embody it. Become one with it. Become the person who is being what you need to be and doing what you need to do to have what you desire. Call it in.

At this point, it's important to notice where old habits try to overtake you, fears, doubts, worries, anything that tries to pull you off center. And deal with it immediately. Keep coming back to this new energetic stance you have created for yourself.

If you do this, what you desire will already be a part of your energy fields. It will already exist around you. It's Universal Law that if you desire something, it does exist for you. Now you're ready to move into action.

"It takes third-dimensional action to create third-dimensional results. It takes massive third-dimensional action to create massive third-dimensional results."

Creating What You Want Uses the Energy of All Three of These

Check in with yourself today. On a scale of 1 – 10, how is your body, your mind, your heart? Creating what you want and allowing it to come to you uses the energy of all three of these.

Since turning my life into an experiment for the Law of Attraction in 2003, I have come to realize that there is a unique perfect balance for me of all three of these integral states of being in order for me to manifest my highest possibilities and maintain what I create.

Each of you will have a blend of these three that works best for you, and it can change and evolve over time or depending on your circumstances. What serves you best is to be aware of each of these and how you engage with and express them in your life. Pay attention to when things are not coming to you, when you are not creating what you are intending, and when you feel stuck or stagnant. That is the time to focus on one of these areas and bring yourself back into a Place Of Power.

Open Heart.

Focused Mind.

Strong Body.

We use our physical body as the vessel through which we create what we want. Our feelings, which we either allow to move through our body or store in our body, affect what we call into our lives. The Universe does not respond to our words. It responds to our feelings. Emotions are energy in motion. We have been equipped with a Feeling Guidance System that is meant to serve us.

We use our mind to focus on what we want and to gain insight and awareness that will create mindset shifts which allow us to call into our lives more of what we want and achieve the transformation we desire.

We use our heart to open and allow in all the good we are calling forth and to love ourselves enough to bring it to us.

Creating what we want, consciously, is a WHOLE experience. We are engaged in this process physically, mentally, emotionally and spiritually.

Spend some time exploring where your strengths and weaknesses lie right now, where you feel balanced and strong and where you feel vulnerable. One or more of these areas may hold repeated patterns of being out of balance. If so, decide what you would like to change and take action. When doing this, take one thing at a time, especially for some of the bigger issues that have been with you longer and have a greater hold on you, the ones that are anchored in your body, mind and heart.

Let me give you an example of how this can play out. In 2007, I opened my first business, a local healing and wellness center in my community. I was so passionate about helping and healing and serving a need I saw in my area that I just began to give and give. I came into this new endeavor with a very open heart. In the process of that, I kept ignoring or avoiding the strategic and financial aspects of my business, and I did not make good decisions. I did not set goals, and I did not get coaching or guidance. When my business was obviously becoming a very expensive hobby, and I had run my personal and family finances into the ground, I realized I had to make a change. At that time, I made the decision to close my business. Very quickly, the Universe provided me another opportunity, a chance to make new decisions and take different actions. This time, I set out with a focused mind, and I made decisions that supported the business much better, but I found that in order for me to do this, I had to close my heart, and my healing business suffered for it. Of course, I looked for the lessons and found a new balance, a new way of being for me, where I could come to my business with both an open heart and a focused mind. My business thrived. I built a full-time private practice. And my clients and students were served in a much higher way. My own life was more satisfying and fulfilling. I also have found that the more my business grows and the more people I serve, I have to be able to hold the energy for all the people I am supporting and guiding. I need to keep my body strong. It's the vessel I rely on to do the work I do.

Look at your daily habits and your daily life and see where you are giving positive attention to each of these; your body, your mind and your heart. Where might you create more balance? What is being routinely neglected? What are you experiencing as a result of this? Imagine how things could change with the changes you are willing to make right now.

My Coach's Request To You: Pick one area – strong body, focused mind, or open heart – and add a significant activity to your daily life that will strengthen this area and bring you more satisfaction.

Chapter Five: M.O.V.E. or Be Moved. It's Always Your Choice.

Many of my clients share that they have this big thing they feel they are called to do in the world. They think they have gifts. They want more fulfillment in their lives. They are experiencing exactly the longing that I knew for so many years before I began living a life of significance and success.

There was a time when I wasn't even sure what I wanted was possible. I was caught up in all my obligations and responsibilities and all the roles I was playing, and it didn't occur to me, yet, that I had created it. All of it. All the busyness in my life? I had created it myself. And then I used it as an excuse not to have what I wanted, be what I wanted and do what I wanted.

What I want to share with you today is that it all starts with making a decision. Yep, you make a decision to create change. You DECIDE to move forward. Those first few steps in this direction can feel like wading in quicksand, but stay with it.

Imagine you are suddenly changing course and turning a huge ship or a giant jet plane. As you build momentum, you are uplifted into a new energy, and everything begins to move in your favor. The key is, you have to take the first step. Before everything shows up!

This is where a lot of my clients get tripped up. Because they are waiting. Waiting for better timing, more money, more security in a relationship, closure in a situation, and any number of things they perceive need attention. We're talking about your WHOLE life here, and all those things will get addressed once you start moving. In fact, a lot of it will begin to take care of itself in what feels like a very natural way. It will move with you.

It drives me crazy to see my clients and students and potential clients and students stuck HERE, in this place. Nothing happens here. Except that it eats away at you.

The best time is always NOW. You hear it. So why don't you believe it? What are you afraid of?

Now, What are YOU meant to take out into the world today?

Those are the two aspects competing for your time, energy and resources. They are battling for it. Which one wins? Whichever one you feed.

Energy never stands still. You are ALWAYS either moving towards or away from what you desire. You make a decision, even with your indecision and inaction. You make a decision to put off your highest good, to turn a deaf ear or a blind eye to what is calling you to come forth. You are here for a purpose. You are a part of the plan. The life of your dreams, a life you love that supports you, is within reach. YOU have to create it. Every day. Consistently, boldly, relentlessly.

It all starts when you Make A Decision, the first step in my M.O.V.E. process for moving forward in any area of your life.

What Decision can you make for your highest good today?

Know Yourself

Whenever you are thinking about making a big life transition, there are really three ways to go about it. Knowing yourself well can make a difference in the amount of stress you experience during this time as well as the amount of success you are able to create.

I talk a lot about taking honest inventory, and this is one of those times when the pay off for doing this consistently can be huge.

You want to pay attention both to the actions you are taking, and not taking, and to the energy you are carrying about it.

When working with clients who come to me ready to make a move or at least considering the possibility, I take some time with them first to explore their hardwiring and their mindset.

I have had clients who have successfully taken big leaps on the spot without much looking back at all and have been able to move forward very quickly without experiencing a lot of fallout. The energy they are holding is that as they go off the side of that cliff, either the road will rise up to meet them or they will grow wings and be taught how to fly. The key to making this work is that they immediately get into massive action and stay in massive action.

Know yourself. If you are not a risk-taker, the stress you may cause yourself in taking the big leap will work against the positive energy you need to "just keep swimming." For these clients, I suggest they determine what I call a tolerate date. They are using up valuable time and energy spinning in how much they don't like where they are and how unhappy they are, and they get into a lot of asking how things might change for them. By setting a date with yourself, the absolute maximum time you are willing to tolerate these circumstances, you stop the mind's endless chatter about it, and you satisfy its need to know.

Now, everything will begin to conspire to work for you toward that goal, and you are no longer working against yourself. As you shift from the negative energy to the positive energy, you begin to be differently and to do things differently, and things start to come together for your benefit. Very often, people end up coming out of their undesirable circumstances much sooner than the date they set, and it happens in a much more natural way.

Then there are those who continue to work with the positive energy of their growing desire. They are visualizing it, feeling it, and sending their order out to the Universe. But they are not taking any action, and they have not set any goals. What most often happens here is that as the desire grows stronger and the feelings associated with it become a part of who you are, the Universe begins to work in your favor in response to your ever-increasing desire. Because you are not taking action, you are not creating space, and you are not letting go of what no longer serves you. What you end up seeing here is the rug being ripped out from under you. This is when you are suddenly forced out of a job, a home, a relationship, or a geographical location.

Each of these is a choice. The more responsibility you are willing to take, the more power you are given over your own life. It is all about becoming conscious and aware and taking action.

What Is My Next Step

You only need to know the next step to take the next step.

Too often, people come to me for coaching, for support and guidance, and they are just sitting and spinning in place because they don't know all the steps. And so they take no steps. I work with both ledge leapers and baby steppers, and it doesn't matter which one you are or what you are most comfortable doing right now, it's all about taking that next step. That is the only way the steps beyond that will show themselves to you.

Don't waste any more time sitting still. You are ready to get moving forward in the direction of your dreams and desires to create a better life now. Know that there are no mistakes, and you cannot fail. You have a tool, Course Correction, that you can use, as you are learning to read feedback from the Universe.

Get into a quiet reflective or meditative state and ask yourself, that part of you that already knows the answers, "What is my next step?"

Remember, you only need to know the next step to take the next step.

Imagine if you are planning on driving from the West Coast to the East Coast. You have a map, so you know the direction you want to move in, and you have a destination where you would like to arrive. Even with a map, you cannot know and plan for every thing that will show up along the way. You trust yourself to make this journey. You are prepared. You have made a decision to go, and you are committed.

Imagine that you are traveling at night. You can only see as far as your headlights shine out in front of you, and you make the journey this way all night long. You cannot, of course, see all the way from the West Coast to the East Coast, and every step you take, every mile you travel, everything is changing in every moment. People are coming and going and may or may not cross your path depending on the decisions and choices you make. You even have a choice of routes to take. You get to determine your speed and whether you want to get there fast or take a more scenic route, whether you want to stop along the way and visit people or places, learn things, or simply rest.

You would not question in the middle of this journey, will I still end up at my destination? Will I be able to get to the East Coast? You would not doubt and turn back out of fear. You would keep moving forward. If you got stuck, you would get help. If you got lost, you would stop and get some better directions.

This journey is much the same.

As you move along, you are changing every minute, with every person and thing that crosses your path, and with every experience you have, all that you encounter. You are different halfway through the journey than you were at the beginning. You have seen different things, thought different things, learned different things, experienced different things, and felt different things, most likely even made some changes in your plans along the way. The longer the journey from here to there, the more this will happen for you.

Delight in the journey. There is so much to experience along the way. Here is a gift for you. Be excited for your journey. Your journey is now and always has been. You have never not been on your journey, on your path. No matter the u-turns, the distractions, the turning back, the side trips and the stops you have made along the way, you are journeying.

The more you can enjoy the journey and being with yourself on this journey, supporting yourself unconditionally, the better it will be for you.

What is my next step? Ask yourself this.

"Remember, even if you're on the right track, you'll get run over if you just sit there."

Here's the important part of this, and every successful person will tell you this, when you receive that next step, you need to move into action. Take that next step. Because once you do, then the next one and the next one and the next one will unfold. Maybe you've heard the saying, "Remember, even if you're on the right track, you'll get run over if you just sit there."

I've been there. Hesitating, not moving, not taking action. Stuck in my stuff. So many of my clients come to me when they are exactly in this place. They get clarity, and they experience desire, then they keep getting in their own way and just sit there while everything around them is trying to come together to support them... if they would just move. That seems to be the place that gets people, that they have to take real physical 3-D action to manifest in this physical world what they want.

Sad to say, I have seen some of my clients and students, and I have experienced myself, the cosmic 2×4 come swinging around while I'm just sitting there. I call this a "brick-to-the-head" moment.

The best part of this is that you just need to take consistent baby steps in alignment with what you have told the Universe and yourself that you want. It's very effective, the baby steps. Just don't stop the momentum by standing still. Act, Assess, Adjust.

Every day, ask yourself, "What is my next step?" Ask yourself, and ask your guidance, and when you get an answer, act on it. Do this every day. Do not miss a day. The more you work with this, the more quickly and frequently the answers will come.

Here's something to know about this, too. Do this, every day. Often, you won't receive the answer right away while you are sitting there waiting for it. Sometimes we have to stop trying so hard, like when you're trying to remember a name so you can tell someone, and then suddenly you can't come up with it at all. So do the asking, then go on with your business for the day. It will come in. Watch for it. Notice every thing that shows up. Expect it. It will come in for you.

A Client Story: This Is How It Works, And I Count On It

My new client was asking the Universe for guidance. She kept feeling the nudging, and she knew a better more Purpose-full life was calling to her. She went to a psychic and had a reading, and there it was, clearly laid out before her, the life she was living now that was less than. And she didn't like it!

She set a powerful intention right then to use the information being shown to her, to shift that energy and change her life. And things began to happen!

"Once you make a decision, the Universe conspires to make it happen." – Ralph Waldo Emerson

I did not know this at the time. What I did know is that she began to be on my mind, and then I received a free ticket to an event I was attending in her city, and I offered it to her. At first, I thought, surely she can't attend. After all, this is during the week, and she works full time, but I followed my inspiration, and I invited her. Turns out, she had just resigned from her job and was available to go.

The event was life-changing for her, and she began to connect the dots. She hired me as her Coach, made a decision to take a scary leap into a Private Coaching Program, and we got started soon after the event was over. And the Universe continued to provide. She has a cousin who contacted her when he found out what she was doing, and he let her know he builds websites and helps with branding and that he was available to help her. She connected with a Teacher at the event and made another decision to study Tarot reading, and people began to show up asking for her services. She is on her way!

Less than 60 days later, she is creating a life she loves and wants to live, a life that will support and sustain her much more than the energy-draining job she decided to leave. She is about to launch her new website, offer her services, and she has a book coming out before the year's end, that she has finally decided to finish. And suddenly it wasn't so hard!

Yesterday, during our session together, I told her, your Guides are telling me to ask you what The Star Tarot card means to you, that there is a message there for you. And that is when she told me about the psychic reading she had. She said that in that reading, The Star card was inverted, meaning it was giving her the opposite of the card's true meaning.

The Star represents for her, "Your Time To Shine. Feeling Good. Feeling Nurtured and Being Able to Nurture Others. Reaching Your Goal." When she was living the reverse of that, she was feeling fear, overwhelmed, and full of doubt.

But she made a decision to do differently, to be differently, and now she is receiving the promise of desires fulfilled. It's her Time To Shine!

This is how it works, and I count on it.

- Pay attention to your desires.

- Make a decision.

- Start taking action.

- Watch for opportunities.

- Follow the breadcrumbs.

- Receive your good.

- Don't Stop!

I love being able to work with my clients intuitively, energetically and strategically all at the same time. It's what has made working with her so powerful and amazing. We work with her gifts and her Guidance, we work with the energy, and then we create strategy to bring her Vision into physical form, so she can make money while making a difference, and so that she can live a Purpose-full life.

She turned it around:

The Star

Upright – Fresh hope and renewal. Healing of old wounds. Hope. renewal of faith and hope. Spiritual love. A mental and physical broadening of horizons. Promise and fulfillment. inspiration. Influence over others. Vigour and confidence. Protection.

Ill   Dignified   or   Reversed   – Self doubt. Stubbornness. Unwillingness or inability to adapt to changing circumstances and accept the opportunities it may bring. Lack of trust and self-doubt. Obstacles to happiness. Diminished life. Inability to freely express oneself. Rigidity of mind.

You can, too!

Chapter Six: What To Do When Your Stuff Comes Up, Because It Will!

What Have I Been Asking For?

When something happens to us that throws us off course or doesn't fit into our plans, we often begin to question.

"Why is this happening to me?"

"What did I do to deserve this?"

"What am I going to do about this?"

The better question to ask would be, "What have I been asking for?"

You see, nothing happens by coincidence. Nothing comes to us without reason. Anything that shows up in our world can only come to us because, in some way, it matches what we are asking for.

We get to ask for whatever we want, and we send that out into the Universe through our feelings and desires. Sometimes, we are using tools that are helping us to consciously create our circumstances, as well. At any time, there exists a continuum, and we are both consciously creating and unconsciously creating.

What we don't orchestrate is the how of it all, and this is where building trust with the All That Is really serves us. Always, there is a bigger picture. We are a part of it, along with everyone and everything else. We ask for what we want, and then the Universe goes to work to deliver it.

Now, here's where things get messy. Many times, I have asked for things in my life, and then when they come about, I am surprised. I mean, I would NEVER orchestrate things to happen that way. That's not the way I envisioned this would go. Yet, as it all unfolds, I do see that what I want is what is coming to me.

A Higher Wisdom is at work here and a Higher Intelligence.

In this same way, I have had times when I have told God exactly what I want and left the how's completely up to Universal Design. Right now is one of those times. Late last year, I started letting God know what I wanted in my life. I really felt it, and I got specific... in the essence of it. I said, I don't know how any of this can or will happen. It's what I want, though. And I went on about my business.

While I was doing what I am here to do, getting up every morning and stepping out into the world, offering what I have, creating value, and being in inspired action, engaged in the cycle of giving and receiving, the Universe began delivering all these incredible things and circumstances to me in ways that I could not have ever dreamed up. I sit here today on the verge of making huge life changes that will bring me immense joy and satisfaction and support the work I am doing in the world and the life I want to live with my husband and my children and my community. And it has been the easiest and most effortless thing to receive. Ever.

I mean, I KNOW this stuff works. I teach it. I coach people through it. It's a way of living for me now. But still, from time to time, I get surprised by the impeccable way this all works.

The Law of Attraction works. It's on all the time. You don't choose to engage with it, do a little manifesting, then turn it off and go back into your toxic relationships, environments, thoughts, habits and patterns.

It all counts. It all matters.

When people come to me in crisis, the first thing I do is have them go back and look at the intentions they have been setting recently and what they have been asking for. Almost immediately, I am able to help them identify patterns and relationships so they see why the things in their life are showing up the way they are. It is always on target.

"Why is this happening to me?" creates a constrictive energy. We turn in on ourselves. We feel victimized. We close ourselves off. We shut down.

"What have I been asking for?" creates an expansive energy that we can work with to move forward. We are not victims. Instead, we are Creators. We are receiving feedback from the Universe, and there is great benefit for us here. What is showing up now is bringing us what we have been asking for. Here is hope. Here is promise. This shift in energy alone lifts us up out of a stagnant space so we can grow.

Many times, what is showing up first is what we need to clear, heal and resolve so that we can receive what we have been asking for.

Try this the next time something shows up that doesn't feel good to you or seems at first glance to be counterproductive to what you are dreaming about and desiring. Examine where your trust lies, in yourself and in your connection to the All That Is.

Then ask yourself, "What have I been asking for?" Open to the answers. They might surprise you.

Get Over Your Garbage and Take Action! What?

Well, I wouldn't have said it quite that way.

A few years ago, I had the opportunity to speak with Janet Switzer, Business Coach to Jack Canfield and many other well-known Transformational Leaders in the Human Potential Movement.

As I was pitching her the work I was developing at the time, she said, "I see what you do." Your message to people is, "Get over your garbage and take action!"

Well? Yes!

I call my work, *Master the Art of Taking Action: Get Moving in the Direction of Your Dreams and Desires and Create A Better Life Now!* In all truth, how I got from where I was to where I am now was by learning how to, indeed, get over my garbage, and then I had to learn how to take action in an empowered and intuitive way that best serves me.

I got to a place in working with my clients where they were beginning to make new discoveries about themselves and their world and creating some powerful shifts in their thoughts and feelings and beliefs. They were getting stuck, though, right at the point where it was time to take action. And that is why I created a body of work focused on how to *Master the Art of Taking Action to Create A Better Life Now!* Yes, I did say, "Now!" And I mean it.

Along this journey, here are some of the things I did that you can do, too:

- Dig deep.
- Chip away at the crap.
- Build Belief.
- Take massive action. Consistently.
- Reclaim your Divine Birth Right.
- Embrace your Purpose.
- Reframe everything.
- Invest in yourself with Teachers, Mentors, Coaches and Spiritual Advisors.
- Allow the shift to happen.
- Uplevel your environments.
- Connect with your passions and Purpose and allow yourself the Creative Expression to integrate them into your everyday life.
- Learn to manage your energy.
- Develop your intuition.
- Be courageous enough to master Emotional Authenticity.
- Get clear with your money.
- Take Honest Inventory.

- Heal your issues that show up around your value, worth, gifts, self-image, need to be liked and self-promotion.
- Recognize Resistance, and don't back down.
- Love Yourself.

As I was working through my stuff and on myself, I kept getting a very clear message, "Are you over yourself yet?" I'd come to a stuck place, and I'd ask, "Why, God, why can't I make this work? What am I missing?" And, again, "Are you over yourself yet?" As I cleared away more and more of the mental and emotional clutter that had become my life, I realized, that is exactly it. Get over your garbage. Get over the constant beating up and second guessing and sabotaging yourself. Get over feeling not enough. You are here, now, and who you are is enough for someone. Your journey is important, and it can have impact on others only when you are willing to share it. I DID get over myself and became my SELF.

These are all a part of the process to *Master the Art of Taking Action*. This is what I work on with my clients and students as I continue to work on this in my own life. It has been life-changing and game-changing. My life now is unrecognizable from the life I was living just 7 years ago and even 5 years ago.

Make A Decision. It all starts right here. The first step in my M.O.V.E. process is M.ake A Decision. As soon as you do, you will set things in motion, and the Universe will conspire on your behalf. You have to take the first step. Every time.

Move from the reactive energy of SCARED to the creative energy of SACRED. All it takes is a little shift. Do you C it?

When you work on your business, your business works on you.

With a bachelor's degree in Advertising and Marketing, a master's degree in Counseling and Guidance, and a Seminary education as a Spiritual Director and a Hospital Chaplain, I bring a real mixed bag when it comes to working with people who are working on their businesses.

We can educate ourselves in all the best and most effective business-building systems, and model ourselves after the most successful people in our industry, and still, at the end of the day, we are often left asking, why do some make it and some don't? If it was just this simple, learn what we need to know, and do it, we'd all be wildly successful.

So we continue to search for the person with THE answer, THE key, the one thing we are missing that will make it all come together for us when we have it. You can stop searching; the key is You. The answer is You. You are the most integral tool in your business and in your life.

The common denominator in everything you set out to do is You, and the differing factor in your business and everyone else doing something just like you, is also You.

What I have discovered while building my own business is this:

When you work on your business, your business works on you.

Now, when you are looking at the snapshot of where your business is right now, today, where are you in that snapshot? Your business is offering you the opportunity to see yourself and to get to know yourself better. Your business is a reflection of your current state of mind. Like any trusted friend, it will showcase your strengths and also help you see where you are standing in your own way, if you are ready to see it.

This involves taking honest inventory and taking responsibility.

Your business is your creation. You as the Creator have put all of you into what you have created, and it is reflecting all of you back.

When we look out at our businesses, we see what is showing up that is exactly what we wanted, and we see what is showing up that we don't want. We put our heart and soul into it, and still, there are those things showing up that we don't want. We are responsible for both.

I believe that inner healing is a strategy for success, and I have applied that to my own life with great results. When we begin to dream big dreams, to set intentions and goals for ourselves, when we begin to strive for prosperity, abundance, health, wealth and success, everything that is not in alignment with that rises up to be healed or transformed. We must heal so that we can soar.

When we have a big vision for our life, we have high desire, and often we encounter high resistance, we find our stuck points. We find ourselves doing what we've always done, not taking new action, stuck on replay. This can result in creating a lot of what we don't want, or feeling like we aren't creating anything at all, along with feelings of anger, frustration, hopelessness, and powerlessness. By not addressing this aspect of our business, we are standing in our own way. Once you start to spin, you find yourself doing the same things over and over again. We have a lot invested in staying here, and sometimes we don't know how to get out.

I have worked for many years now with people who find themselves stuck in inaction, standing in their own way. This causes all kinds of dissatisfaction and unhappiness, and eventually it can turn to anger at yourself or negative self-talk or feelings of wanting to just give up or beating yourself up. People try to make changes for short periods of time, then they get uncomfortable, and they retreat back into what is familiar and known, even if it isn't good for them.

The first thing you can do for yourself and your business is to show up in a different way. Take ownership of your business and your business's owner, YOU. Take responsibility for all of your creation, and be open to what you might find. Then begin taking honest inventory.

Just showing up for yourself and being willing to do this will start shifting you out of where you no longer want to be and open a space for powerful movement.

Stop Beating Yourself Up

In my work, I help people to live their extraordinary instead of their wounding. It's a powerful paradigm shift, and it changes everything.

There's a story I love, and I want to share it with you now, because it's a beautiful illustration of this work, living your extraordinary instead of your wounding.

A grandson told of his anger at a schoolmate who had done him an injustice. Grandfather said: "Let me tell you a story." "I, too, have felt a great hate for those that have taken so much, with no sorrow for what they do. But, hate wears you down and does not hurt your enemy. It is like taking poison and wishing your enemy would die. I have struggled with these feelings many times. It is as if there are two wolves inside me: one is good and does no harm. He lives in harmony with all around him and does not take offense when no offense was intended. He will only fight when it is right to do so, and in the right way. But the other wolf is full of anger. The littlest thing will set him into a fit of temper. He fights with everyone, all the time, for no reason. He cannot think because his anger and hate are so great. It is hard to live with these two wolves inside me, for both of them try to dominate my spirit." The boy looked intently into his grandfather's eyes and asked, "Which one wins, Grandfather?" The grandfather solemnly replied, "The one I feed."

Our ego is fed easily, every day. It is triggered by our wounds, and when we act from those wounds, it does not serve us well. Our Spirit wants to be fed, too, and we often do this most when we have extra time or extra money or when things get really tough for us. How wonderful is it when we can feed our Spirit on a regular basis? It grows stronger and stronger. You have to exercise your spiritual "muscles," too.

I am a busy person with a full life. I am a mother and a wife, a volunteer in my community, and a businesswoman. Sometimes I overcommit. Sometimes I run myself too much. Sometimes my priorities get out of whack. Unexpected things have a way of dropping into my lap. At the same time, my spirituality is very important to me. I have lived with that part of my life shut down or put on hold while I went about the business of everyday life, until I realized that was not good for me. I have gone off on extended spiritual quests where I put my physical life and my physical world in the background, and what happens? People and things start acting out, calling for my attention. My children act out, my pets get sick or misbehave, bills aren't getting paid on time, things around my house start breaking or malfunctioning. You know what I mean?

I have worked for many years now with people who are stuck in inaction. This causes all kinds of dissatisfaction and unhappiness and eventually turns to anger at yourself or negative self-talk or feelings of wanting to just give up or beating yourself up. People try to make changes for short periods of time, then they get uncomfortable, and they retreat back into what is familiar and known, even if it isn't good for them.

The Ego grows stronger, and the Spirit is weak. Do you know that feeling?

The Ego is just doing it's job, working only with what it knows from past experience, and it's job is to keep you safe and comfortable. That is why it is so important to feed the Spirit.

My passion in more recent years has not just been to work with people who are stuck but to work with people who have a big vision, people who know they are meant to be doing something, people who want to create a life they love, people who desire to do work they love and come from a heart-centered place. People who desire to live a physical life that is spiritually rich. If only they could... get unstuck.

We get stuck in that place of limiting beliefs, toxic emotions, toxic relationships and environments, unhealthy patterns and negative self-talk.

When we begin to dream big dreams, to set intentions and goals for ourselves, when we begin to strive for prosperity, abundance, health, wealth and success, everything that is not in alignment with that rises up to be healed or transformed. We must heal so that we can soar.

In other words, our "stuff" comes up.

Once I began teaching and speaking to groups about these principles, I got asked the same question over and over again. "What do I do when my stuff comes up?" Great question!

I have several things I do when my stuff comes up. I have been filling my spiritual toolbox, and I dig in and start using my energetic processes, tools and techniques to create a shift in my energy which will create movement for me. These processes and tools and techniques also help me feel and interpret my energy and my environment and manage my energy. When you are going down that black hole or are stuck in that dark tunnel is not the time to try surfing the internet or trying to find help. You want to be building and filling your spiritual toolbox and using these processes, tools and techniques on a regular basis, so you are stronger and so they are there to support you when you need them most. The more you use them, the easier it gets, and the more you are able to live in the flow.

Now, you can really starting getting a glimpse of your extraordinary. Now, you can really start accessing your extraordinary and living your extraordinary.

Of course, I do have my own trusted advisors, coaches, teachers and mentors that I know are there for me, and I have learned when it is time to go to them to help me. But because I am doing my own work, I can go with more clarity and focus, know what I need and want, and really benefit from the work they do with me. I now have tools I can use to make this work even more powerful, working on my own after my work with them is complete.

People often come to me when they are in crisis. In the middle of a crisis, it is much more difficult to get things shifting and moving for the better when the person does not have access to any of these tools or an understanding of working with their energy and intuition. I can see the difference, and the first thing I do once I have gotten them into a more stable-feeling place is to begin to lead them through and teach them some processes, tools and techniques they can use and give them homework they can leave with. Hopefully, they will then go home and begin filling their spiritual toolbox and better developing their spiritual practice.

I help people live their extraordinary instead of their wounding, to respond to life in a conscious way, rather than reacting, to become a Conscious Creator, creating a life you love.

I am so committed to this. I am so committed to supporting you in this.

When we have a big vision for our life, we have high desire, and often we encounter high resistance. We find ourselves doing what we've always done, not taking new action, stuck on replay. Do you feel that you are living a life that is dictated by where you've been, toxic emotions, your stories, and negative self-talk? This can result in creating a lot of what you don't want - along with feelings of anger, frustration, hopelessness, and powerlessness. Once you start to spin, you find yourself doing the same things over and over again. We have a lot invested in staying here, and sometimes we don't know how to get out.

Wouldn't you love to stop beating yourself up over inaction? You can when you learn to shift your energy and shift your life.

This Work Requires Extreme Self-Care

I have been traveling a lot over the past 12 months. I love being able to combine pleasure and work all in one trip, like when I was able to visit my daughter and then attend a business conference, and when I was able to attend a MasterMind with my Coach then spend my birthday in a resort on Miami Beach, having the whole day all to myself. That means, I spend time serving myself and then I spend time serving others.

I've been on a lot of airplanes, so I have watched the safety presentation many, many times. I've seen this information so many times in my life, that I find myself zoning out, staring off into space, and that is when I do some of my best thinking.

On a recent trip, as the flight attendant demonstrated the cabin losing pressure and the oxygen mask dropping and began giving instructions, I found myself thinking about this in relation to my business and my life.

Those of us who are called to be healers and to help other people often do so at our own expense. You will find me constantly speaking to all the helpers of the world about self-care, and I promise you that I practice what I preach. I didn't always.

Think of this as it relates to your own life and to how you show up in the world. As you are building your business or working for your employer or volunteering in your community, are you serving yourself before you go out and serve others?

When you are worn out, drained of energy and running out of oxygen, you cannot fully show up as all of who you are to serve others. This leads to a lot of burn out and frustration, resentment, and feelings of defeat, until no one is being served well.

You are the only one who has the power to change this. Schedule time for yourself into your day, your week, your month and your year. How much time are you willing to schedule off for yourself now? I mean, mark it on your calendar, and commit the time for yourself before you see what else might be calling for your attention.

Then, once you've scheduled the time for yourself, decide what you'd like to do with that time. When was the last time you had a massage, went out for lunch, saw a movie or spent uninterrupted hours in your favorite bookstore?

All of this breathes life back into you, so that you can do your work in the world. Your life will be enhanced, and the lives of those you serve will be enhanced. Everybody wins!

I have learned over the past few years to spend the first few days of the year scheduling all my time off for the year. That is the first thing to go into my calendar. A few years back, my Coach asked me and each of my colleagues, how much time did you schedule off for yourself next year? AND are you committed to keeping these important appointments with yourself... NO MATTER WHAT?!

Hmmm. A couple of years ago, this would have made me squirm. Big Time! But... what about... what if... I don't know yet... Please, put the brakes on your runaway mind right now!

I am a recovering co-dependent, a wounded healer. I have run myself into the ground trying to rescue and save others. I once wanted my life to play out like a Lifetime movie with me as the valiant hero fighting for the helpless and hopeless. I worked harder than the people I was trying to help. I destroyed my health, my finances and my relationships along the way. I became bitter and resentful. I was frustrated, and I lost hope.

Over the past few years, I have learned so much. I have been willing to look at my life, how I'm living it, and what I want it to look like. First. Everything else gets designed, then, to create and support this. That is why we set out to create our own businesses, after all. For the promise of Freedom!

That year, about mid-way through, I began to gift myself with Fridays off, and it made a huge difference for me. Before that, I was trying to eek out time for myself when I had little breaks in my schedule, but I wasn't committed to it, and I let other things intrude. Once I marked that time out for me on a consistent basis, I began taking a yoga class and gave myself time and space to dream and reflect and create without the demands of others. The time is mine to do whatever I want with it.

I am taking care of myself so that I can serve you better.

My Coach's Request To You: Make time for yourself. Give to yourself. Don't make this something that you do after everything and everyone else gets their piece. Give yourself some time and space to breathe. Mark it on your calendar, and honor the gift.

Answer this question, "What do I want my life to look like?" and then M.O.V.E. forward. With this question answered first, making decisions becomes a whole lot easier.

Make this the year you respond to your Highest Good, first, in all areas of your life! Pull out your calendar, and get started right now.

Notes:

Chapter Seven: This Is What I Have, and I'm Here Now

Are You Going To Show Up For This?

I love learning from stories, analogies and parables. I thrive when I plug into people who are where I want to be, have what I want to have and are doing what I want to do and I am able to share their journey and hear their stories and apply them to my own life. Because of this, I offer my life as an experiment and a lesson for others, as well.

Over the years, I have heard to the story of the feeding of the masses many times. It's a staple of Sunday School and Vacation Bible School and can always be counted on to create a powerful sermon. It's a story of a miracle, and who doesn't love a story of a miracle? Hollywood depends on it.

Usually, in this story, the focus is on Jesus. Jesus took 5 loaves and 2 fish, 5 loaves and 2 fish, and he fed the masses. He made enough out of not enough.

Okay, but what happened before that?

Do you know how you can hear or see or experience something more than once, and you will find the nuggets when you need them, and when you have the eyes to see and the ears to hear? You know when you watch a movie again or read a book or listen to an audio, and you hear or see something different, something that you didn't know was there before? That is how it was for me recently. I was really looking when this little story came my way, and I had the eyes and the ears to see and hear something very different. It came in the way of this very simple story, and the impact has been huge.

I want to focus on the boy. This boy, who probably was brought along to this exact place on this day, maybe by others, maybe of his own accord. He might have known he was going to see something exciting, something special, but was he able to glimpse even a little what an integral role he would play in this event?

The boy was there when someone noticed that the people were tired and hungry. The boy was a part of the crowd that was calling for someone to provide for them. Everyone was looking around. Who will bring food for us all? The logical answers would be to look to the leaders of the community, the organizers of the event, or the wealthy townspeople who might donate something to those in need.

The boy was standing there with 5 loaves and 2 fish, looking out upon this great crowd. He had to know there wasn't enough, and yet no one else was stepping forward to offer a solution.

And then he showed up. This is what I have, and I'm here now.

He didn't let "Who am I?," "What do I have to offer?," "I don't have enough," or "I'm not ready" stand in his way. He showed up.

How many times in our lives do we say, "I'm not ready yet," when an opportunity presents itself? How often do we think, "I don't have enough to make a difference"?

Many of us have heard the quote attributed to both Nelson Mandela and Marianne Williamson, which asks, "Who am I to be brilliant, gorgeous, talented, fabulous?" And then, "Who are you not to be?"

The Universe supports Action. Every moment counts. Every moment there's a choice point. The integral piece of your life in every moment is You. You are the force behind what happens in your life. Don't let things just happen to you. Don't look around seeing a need and waiting for someone else, someone better or more qualified, to step up. You step up, you step out, and the Universe steps in to meet you.

We cannot know the full picture, the effect we will truly have. We don't need to. The boy had 5 loaves and 2 fish – this is what I have, and I'm here now – and he showed up. The Supernatural took care of the rest.

One of the most important guiding principles I ever learned was Leave the How's to the Universe. I show up as I am with what I have. I show up in every moment, every day. And from right where I am, I offer what I have. This creates an energy that activates the full support of the Universe. Lives are changed. Among them, mine. Profoundly.

A beloved Coach I had several years ago challenged me to fully live this way, and I took it to heart. She told me to believe that in every moment you have everything you need to do what you are here to do. Bring all you have and all you are to every moment. Offer it, and allow the Universe to take it and weave it into the greater whole.

You have something to offer, and you're here now.

Ready! Set! What?

Picture this. You're on the set. Everything has been staged just as you imagined. All the players have shown up and been given their roles. Now, that moment, a pause, as all energies come together into a very clear focus. You are leaning into it.

The Director shouts, "Ready! Set! Action!"

What gets everything and everyone in motion? Action!

Google "action" and "success" and see for yourself what every successful entrepreneur and every powerful spiritual leader has to say about it.

Here's one I found: "Success seems to be connected with action. Successful people keep moving." — Conrad Hilton

Action is the lynchpin of the whole manifestation process. Nothing happens without it.

Oh, yeah, you might experience the good feelings. There's a high that comes from visualizing and dreaming. But your results remain in your head and are expressed through your thoughts and feelings. It is not until you take action that things show up here in your physical world.

I always say, do the energetic work first! It saves so much time. But don't stop there. You still have to take action.

I have made a living this year out of helping people master the art of taking action. Why? Because people get stuck just before this step. They get frozen, feel paralyzed. And so they do nothing. And then they get nothing. A year goes by, and they are still in the same place they were 365 days before. They still have what they've always had, but it's painful, because they still have the dreams and desires for something more. Those didn't go away.

Haven't you been getting ready and set long enough? Isn't it time to dive in?

There has never been a better time than now. There never will be.

What I discovered was that it's really easier than I thought. Much of it was in my mind. Once I got into action, I found that if I just stayed in action, I could take baby steps, and I could create profound results. And I have been doing that now specifically and consistently for 3 ½ years, and it has made all the difference in my world.

You are always, ALWAYS, either moving towards or away from your goal, your vision, your mission, your truth and the life of your dreams. In every moment there is a choice point to get into action or to retreat. Do not fool yourself into thinking that standing still will not have an impact. There is no true "still." In every moment, you are making choices that are either moving you towards or away from what you want and where you want to be. Not taking action IS an action.

My Coach's Request To You: Identify something you want that isn't showing up for you right now or something you don't want that is showing up for you. Make a decision to take one action that will move you toward where you want to be. Then take Action!

If you find that you are experiencing resistance, if you feel that you need support and guidance to move, I am here.

Going From Resistance to Receptivity

You, the possibility seeker, you know what you want, even if it's not clearly defined yet, even if you are just starting to step into it, just starting to open the door and take a peek at the possibilities for your life that are beginning to call out to you. You may not know what you want yet, but you know you want SOMETHING. Something more? Something different?

We hear that call, we consider the possibility of stepping into our greatness, we begin to embrace our true purpose, and as soon as we really do that, it seems that we encounter obstacles and crisis. They feel like they are getting in our way and blocking our path.

What if I told you that they really are a beautiful sign that you are exactly where you are meant to be doing exactly what you are meant to be doing? What if I told you they are signaling to you, you've got it, you're so close, keep going?

When we don't know this, we get stuck. We come into contact with our big dream, start setting intentions and goals for ourselves, and begin to strive for the good things like freedom, prosperity, abundance, health, wealth, and success, and, ultimately, living an authentic life... we begin to invest the commitment and effort, and then we come to a screeching halt in the face of what shows up first. We lose momentum, wonder if it's worth it, and fall back into what is comfortable and safe.

Notice, though, that I said, what comes first. It does come first. The stuff. But it's a necessary and integral part of the process, and once you understand it, you can use it to create magnificent results.

As soon as it happens, all you want to do is get unstuck, recover your momentum, and move powerfully into your greatest vision for your life, right?

I have been there, a possibility seeker, with dreams and desires growing stronger within me, calling me to step out into my greatness and embrace and live my purpose. I sought out teachers and mentors. I trained in many healing modalities. I developed my intuition. I turned my life into an experiment with The Law of Attraction. I studied the business practices of successful Spiritual Entrepreneurs. There is a lot of talk out there, an information overload, but who is really putting it into action and getting results?

I want you to know that as you begin to explore the mastery of your two greatest and most powerful tools – your energy and your intuition – and using them in your day-to-day life in a focused and purposeful and in a meaningful and conscious way, you will transform your life.

When we work with our energy and intuition, we can create shift that moves us out of struggle, out of spinning our wheels, out of falling back into patterns that no longer serve us. We put energy into action, and we get results.

When the resistance shows up – the "dissonance" as one of my coaches likes to call it, "your stuff," as I call it – if you struggle with it, you place yourself energetically into a Victim role. Things happen to me. Things get in my way. They are difficult to overcome. I am trying so hard. I have no control. I guess I'm not meant to do this. I can talk about this, because I have run every one of those programs. And they all got me nowhere.

When we use this feedback from the Universe and take responsibility for everything that shows up, yes, all of it, suddenly we have tools to work with, and we are in control of our own lives. Now we energetically step into the role of Creator. Now we can consciously create a life we love!

It shows up first, this stuff, so that you can get really clear on what is ready to be consciously dealt with, to be healed or cleared or embraced. It tells you exactly what no longer serves you and shows you what you need to let go of, right here, right now, to step into the intentions you have set for yourself, to be, do and have what you are telling the Universe you want.

When we begin to dream big dreams, to set intentions and goals for ourselves, when we begin to strive for prosperity, abundance, health, wealth and success, everything that is not in alignment with that rises up to be healed or transformed. We must heal so that we can soar.

Don't let this part of the process get you stuck in inaction. This causes all kinds of dissatisfaction and unhappiness and eventually turns to anger at yourself or negative self-talk or feelings of wanting to just give up or beating yourself up.

Use this part of the process of manifesting to get unstuck, recover your momentum, and to move powerfully into your greatest vision for your life. Suddenly, your path becomes clearer, your journey easier and more effortless, and most importantly, fulfilling and joyful.

Could there really be a way to experience relief and freedom in your own life that truly works? I say, yes, definitely.

This principle, when considered and integrated into your life, can create a paradigm shift for you that will begin to shift your energy, and, therefore, shift your life!

Notes:

Notes:

Chapter Eight: Holding Steady While It All Goes to Hell

"Where are we going and why am I in this handbasket?"

It always makes me sad when I have a client right there at a breakthrough who no-shows her next appointment. I know that means she is right there, doing the work, and things are changing. But she doesn't always know that. She is knee-deep in the discomfort and the pain, suddenly feeling like she's fighting for her life. And in this moment, nothing could be more appealing than going back to the familiar, and numbing out.

Right this moment, everything in your world exists because it is an energetic match to you. It is in alignment with your energy. When you change, your energy shifts, and everything and everyone around you responds to it.

This can show up as people who suddenly start getting irritated or upset or being very emotional around you. Your children may act out. Your pets may get sick. Things in your home may start breaking down. I have had all of these things happen to me.

I find this particularly happens when I go away to a conference or retreat where I am doing a lot of inner work and shifting into new awareness and insight. Two years ago, I attended a conference that changed me profoundly and shifted the path of my business, as well. When I came home from that trip, my husband was a wreck over a bunch of little things, one of my children was acting out, and my dog was sick all night long up on my return. Within the next two weeks, two of my air conditioning units broke down, and then my water heater went out.

During that time what you need to do most is often the most challenging thing to do. You need to hold your energy in that new space. You need to center and ground and stay put while all chaos swirls around you. When you do that, you allow everyone and everything to resettle in new energetic alignment with you, and you hold the change you have worked for. If you can hold steady for two weeks, things will shift again in your favor. And the payoff will arrive.

Unfortunately, what we often do and what I did for many years was read this wrong. You think, I must not be meant to move in this direction. I'm obviously not supported by Spirit in this. My timing is off; I should try again when everyone else is in a better space.

I had a wonderful Coach who taught me about this at the time I was going crazy in my world. She calls it Dissonance. I also talk about it as Resistance. Once you know what it is, and you can expect it, you can be more free to move forward. Use what is happening around you as tools for transformation. My coach's help at this time was invaluable. Because of it, I have changed so much of my life in the past three years and created it like I want it.

It can feel awful, I know. But it doesn't have to.

When you don't know this, you can get stuck. Just as you are coming into contact with your big dream, have started setting intentions and goals for yourself, and are beginning to really reach toward the good things like freedom, prosperity, abundance, health, wealth, and success, and, ultimately, living an authentic life… you begin to invest the commitment and effort, and then come to a screeching halt in the face of what shows up first. This causes you to lose momentum, wonder if it's worth it, and fall back into what is comfortable and safe.

Notice, though, that I said, what comes first. It does come first. The stuff. But it's a necessary and integral part of the process, and once you understand it, you can use it to create magnificent results.

Now I know it's a beautiful sign that I am exactly where I am meant to be, doing exactly what I am meant to be doing. I take it as a sign that I've got this, I am so close. It helps me keep going.

And so, when my clients come to me and tell me that all hell has broken loose in their lives, we look at it together, and I tell them, you're doing the work! You're so close, maybe just three feet from gold. Keep going! Hold steady for a couple of weeks. Center and ground, claim your new energetic space, then allow everyone and everything else to come into new resonance with you.

Don't let this part of the process get you stuck in inaction. Use this part of the process of manifesting to get unstuck, recover your momentum, and to move powerfully into your greatest vision for your life. Suddenly, your path becomes clearer, a way opens for you, and you can see the possibilities before you. By learning to transform your resistance into powerful tools for transformation, you can move forward into allowing and receiving all that you desire and deserve.

Overcome Fear by Moving From Scared to Sacred

I heard an interesting little story once about a man who had a dream that Fear was chasing him. He ran and ran but to no avail – Fear was right on his heels. Finally, exhausted, the man stopped running, turned, looked Fear dead in the face and said: "I give up. You got me. Now what are you going to do to me?" – To which Fear softly responded: "I haven't the slightest idea. This is YOUR DREAM."

One little shift is all it takes to begin to create profound positive change in your life. A small shift in thinking, and then another, and another, until you are thinking new thoughts, doing things differently, and being a greater version of you.

Look at the word Scared, and it may feel like a huge jump from being scared to creating sacred success, the success that comes from making a living doing something you love that creates a sense of significance in your life, allows you to live your purpose, to bring your vision, your mission, your dreams and your truth to the table. You create a lifestyle and a life you love that supports you.

Scared and Sacred. Same letters. But when arranged differently, it makes all the difference.

Imagine you are playing a game of Scrabble, and you have all the letters in front of you.

AECDRS

When you look at the letters, what do you see? One person sees Scared. Another sees Sacred.

And you set about to build your word based on what you see, and you play the game with it.

So much of how you experience your life is perception. Everything comes through a filter, and that filter is you.

It takes time and energy to begin to shift your mindset. At first, it feels like work, something you have to pay attention to. And then, suddenly, you are looking at the scrambled letters and seeing Sacred more than Scared, and then you are seeing Sacred almost all of the time.

Each person looks at the pieces of their own life and sees what they are expecting to see.

Maybe you've heard, FEAR is just False Evidence Appearing Real. Well, it's true. The problem with Fear is that we have created a world in which we've lost the ability to use it as it was intended, a part of our feeling guidance system that puts us into fight or flight so we can fight the tiger in the bushes. Kill it or run away. Instead, we have created an endless supply of "tigers in the bushes" that we now have to deal with every day. Our bodies stay in a constant fight or flight coping pattern, and we burn ourselves out, we become absolutely exhausted.

Creating is challenging when we aren't able to begin from a vibration of Joy and when we can't summon the creative energy we need. Fear is simply a form of resistance. Recognize it for what it is, then get clear, centered, focused and moving. Bring more Joy into your life, right now, right away.

If you are ready to move out of the fear that holds you back and move forward into a life of significance and success, to create sacred success for yourself, here are some things you can do.

10 Touchstones to Freedom to step into who you are and take that out into the world

1. Get back into your own energy

Some of you are more familiar with this, and other people I find really don't fully understand or know what their own energy feels like, especially people who are empathic and intuitive and have been throughout their lives and pick up other people's stuff and carry it around and have even agreed to carry big family energy secrets and stories and programs and beliefs and pattern.

This is something that is really good to do, start doing every day, spending time in your own energy and it's very beneficial right before you go to bed and you kind of let go and disconnect from everything that's going to zap your energy, that's going to drain you and you spend time sleeping and rejuvenating in your own energy.

2. Use your tools

Tools for transformation are many. Choose what you will use, what resonates for you. Don't get into overwhelm trying to apply everything.

My Coach's Request To You: Choose one tool that you already have and use it for 30 days. The key is that you are the integral tool – you learning to use your energy and your intuition to take charge of your life.

Start building a toolbox full of tools that you can use before you get into crisis. These are tools that you can build into your daily spiritual practice. Identify your tools and USE what you have. Plug into a community, a tribe, to learn and share and grow. Know who to go to for help when you need it. This can be a trusted counselor, spiritual advisor, chiropractor, acupuncturist, pastor, mentor, coach, teacher or guide.

3. Clear the way

Your Intuition is there for you. It's coming in all the time, but your mental and emotional clutter are blocking you from receiving guidance and confusing you. Do the inner work, and watch your outer world shift. Stop trying to change everyone and everything, and, instead, change the filter it all comes through. This changes everything!

Begin with a reflection: ask yourself, what is one thing that is showing up in my life that I don't want or one thing that is not showing up in my life that I do want? How does that make you feel? When have you felt like that before? What does it look like on the outside? Who are all the people who play out similar things throughout your life?

Begin to identify patterns. This will lead you to your core issues. We each have just a few core issues that run everything in our lives, how we think, what we believe, what we do or don't do, how we react. At first glance, often people come to me with this long list of all these things that are going on in their lives causing them discomfort and pain, and they don't see how they are all connected, they can't immediately see the patterns. With new awareness, suddenly you can see what is playing out, and then you are that much closer to changing it. Once you change from within, it stops showing up in your outer world. It really does. This is what I do with people every day.

4. Baby Step through it if you have to; just stay in motion!

Small steps create profound change, get started now, do something every day. That is why it is so important to get clear about what you want, what you really want, and where you want to be. You only need to know the destination you want right now, not the how. Get clear about your vision, your mission, your dreams and your truth. Allow this to be pleasurable. Spend time in this energy. Do not stress about it. This isn't a one-time answer, and you are not locked into what you choose right now. This will evolve as you do.

If you want to learn to more about how to do this, go through my 21-Day Email Course I have provided for you at the end of this book.

It is so important to get into motion and stay in motion. Don't stop and start the energy. That takes a lot to get it flowing again.

5. Become a match for what you desire

Work with the essence of what you want. Begin with that, really feel it and connect to it. Choose one thing or condition, and work with it for 30 days.

6. Manage your mindset

Einstein really said it best: "We cannot solve our problems with the same thinking we used when we created them." You just can't create something new with your old way of thinking. New results require new thinking, which creates new energy, which leads to new action.

7. Break free of what limits you

As you begin to do these things and to consciously engage, you will really begin to see what is no longer serving you, and you will begin to make decisions about what to let go of. As you work on empowering beliefs, you will experience the limiting beliefs that once held you back, and now they have lost their power. Once you name them and claim them, they lose their hold on you. As you allow the new in, it becomes important to release the old and let go of toxic environments, relationships, habits, and ways of being that are no longer in alignment with who you are becoming and where you are going.

8. Connect with your Vision, your Mission, your Dreams and your Truth

These things were placed within you for a reason. They are the best clues to help you get started moving in the direction of your dreams and desires to create a better life now. What positively charges you? What lights you up? What are you drawn to? What do you love to do? What are you best at? Why do you feel you are here? What keeps you up at night. Often, where we see a problem or issue, where we keep asking why nothing is being done about it, we are being called to do something ourselves. When we think of something, search for it and don't find it, then wish it existed, it is often for us to create ourselves.

9. Give yourself full permission

The very first two steps of my M.O.V.E. process are Make A Decision and Own It. There is great power in commitment. Once you make a decision, support yourself 100%. Self-doubt, second-guessing, confusion, and beating yourself up waste precious creative energy.

10. Leap so you can Soar

There is a great proverb that says, when we come to the edge of all we know and are about to take the leap into the unknown, we must know that one of two things will happen — there will be something solid for us to stand on, or we will grow wings and be taught how to fly. This is Faith, and it comes from boldly preparing for this moment, for becoming the Master of your life and experience.

Do the energetic work first. Clear the mental and emotional clutter. Let the inspiration flow. When you get the inspired thought, take immediate action. M.O.V.E.
You're sitting on a gold mine. The treasure has been within you all this time. Fear is simply a form of resistance. Recognize it for what it is, then get clear, centered, focused and moving.

Doing Your Part In The Trust Fall

This happens to me a lot. I get contacted by people I have heard from before. I recognize them from my community, they may have come and heard me speak somewhere, and they are attracted to what I have to offer them. Something in them is telling them that I can help. Yet, they come and go, and they never make a decision, and they never commit. I may not see or hear from them for up to a year, then they come back again, still drawn, still speaking to their desires and dreams, and they ask me, how, how can I make this happen? I want to, but...

I want to share with you what I responded to someone who contacted me recently: *Hi, it's great to hear from you. Here is what I have to tell you. It is about making a decision and making a commitment to yourself, then watching for the opportunities to show up to create the means to make it happen. As long as you are holding the energy and coming from the place of, I will when... you will continue to wait until... There just really is no substitute for deciding to do it. I remember hiring my first coach and being so scared, how was I going to pay that every month, where would it come from, but it did come every month, and I have not been without a coach since. Let me know how I can serve you.*

I see this so often, and I really wish I had another answer, I really wish I could tell you to just sit tight and the money will come streaming in. When? When the Universe feels you are ready? You tell the Universe when you are ready. When Spirit thinks you can handle it? If the desire exists within you, then the means to attain it is already here; it already exists. When things are better? When you are stronger? You get better and stronger by being in it, by doing it and growing and evolving along with what you are creating. It is a totally organic process, and you have to be engaged in it for it to work. Are you waiting until you are more prepared, have made time for it, cleared your major obligations, don't have so much you need to do for everybody else? You will always have things in your life, and stuff will always come up. These things show up over and over again as a response, as a match to the energy you are holding in your thoughts, beliefs, actions and repeated patterns.

So, what are you really waiting for?

I'd like to share an experience with you that I had in hopes that I can give you a true feel for what the energy feels like that will get you there. I want you to understand what energy you need to hold to make it happen. In my M.O.V.E. process, I start everything with having you Make A Decision and then owning it 100%. And there's a reason for that.

When I'm talking about making that decision and owning it, visualizing it, and executing it, I want to give you this example. It was so powerful. I love how it showed up. A friend of mine was doing this extreme confidence boot camp, and I was one of the teachers in it. I love when I'm the teacher and, of course, I get to be the student, and I get to be challenged. I get the opportunity to walk my talk. I love how that is.

Part of this involved this ropes course, and I had no fear about it. They had this two-story building with a set up, and you're up on tight ropes, you're harnessed, there's zip lines, you're walking on all these obstacles. I had no fear about any of that.

There's this one thing I had tremendous fear and doubt about, and that was the trust fall. A big part of this kind of boot camp is that the way you do anything is the way you do everything and it all shows up. And you learn physically, mentally, emotionally really by going through these different exercises and working with that group dynamic. What you really feel in the world and how you show up in the world will show up in this experience. I surprised myself with this trust fall; it just terrified me. And it was beautiful, because we did it right before I was to teach this exact thing that I'm presenting now.

I give this talk all the time, all over, about mastering the art of taking action, about making a decision, the importance of committing fully to it and supporting yourself 100%, and this day I was giving this talk. So the instructor said, "It's time for the trust fall." Basically, everyone in your group is standing in two lines facing each other and just holding out their arms. We were a group of mostly women that day. There are these steps leading up to this platform, and you are going to climb up the steps, turn your back to the group, and they've created this cradle with their arms, and you are going to fall backwards into their arms. Very quickly, I realized several things.

I told you, I'm a huge risk taker. I don't mind taking risks, but the risks I take, I'm counting on myself. I know I have everything I need, and I have everything in place, so this to me felt like a risk. I can't even see the people, I don't know if they're going to catch me, I believe they have the intention to catch me, I trust them that much. But I don't know if they will. Can you begin to see how this might have played out first in my early life then continued as I carried this energy with me?

I've been bonding with them all day. I don't know if they can catch me, and I don't know if I want to count on that. Suddenly, it was a risk I did not want to take. I'm falling backwards into the unknown. All these things started coming up for me, and when I started teaching this material afterwards, it all came together.

I want you to think about this. I let a lot of people go ahead of me, not knowing if I would even do this at all, and when she told me it was my turn, "Michelle you're doing this," I had not yet made the decision. In that moment, part of it was that pressure of, I'm getting ready to teach these people something, all eyes are on me. It was a beautiful chance for me to be vulnerable in a powerful way and make it a teaching moment while I was experiencing it myself.

So in this moment, I made the decision. Going up those steps, I still did not know if I was truly going to do this, if I had it in me. But there comes a point where you have to make a decision, and this is the part I really want you to understand. Climbing up those steps, I was saying, "Yeah, there are going to be some consequences if I choose not to do it. Nothing bad is going to happen to me, but I really want to come through for myself, I really want to do this, and I feel like I need to do it."

You need to get comfortable with getting uncomfortable, and that's something I'm always telling my clients and students, so guess what? Again, I have to walk my talk. They were all getting uncomfortable in all kinds of ways throughout the day. This was my moment. When you get to the top, you turn away from the crowd, and they have given you this very specific way you have to stand. You have to cross your arms, you have to straighten your body, your legs have to be a certain way, and your feet, and you assume this position before you fall.

So in that moment, I had to make a decision and own it and then I had to visualize myself doing it, and then I'm going to execute it. All of this happened in a matter of minutes. There was no room for second guessing or doubting, because once you make the decision and you start that momentum backwards, which is, you start the action, if you come out of that position, you're going to hurt the people who are trying to catch you, you're going to hurt yourself, and it becomes dangerous. Perfect setup for me. It was a moment where, once I made the decision, I had to support myself 100%. There was no way to stop myself once I set this in motion. I knew that. I could feel it the moment I got into this position, and I said, "In a moment, I'm going to fall backwards. I cannot stop myself."

Once I start falling, I cannot say, oh, not doing this, and if I let anything get in my way and I come out of the position, I'm going to hurt people that are trusting me, and I'm going to get hurt. I took so much from that about this moving forward work I am teaching you now. What a great way to really get it. I think of that every time I'm going to make a decision now – then I own it, visualize it and execute it 100% as if there is no turning back and no stopping mid-air.

You have got to do it at 100%. If you come in and out of it, it's damaging. It's damaging to you, it's damaging to the other people involved. What if you went into everything you did in that way?

Without all the push- pull energy, the in then out energy, the stopping and starting energy. I really want you to think about the commitment. And if commitment is an issue for you, if it feels scary, if you can't hold it for a long period of time, commit for an hour, commit for 24 hours, just start committing and stick with it.

Now is the time to start. Wherever you are, whatever your life and world are about right now, you will know what your next steps are. Synchronicities will begin to occur if you open up to them. Someone, something will show up and open you up and positively charge you, and you will have the opportunity to step into it.

The Universe Don't Play That Game : A True Story

I know this stuff. I teach this stuff. I Coach my clients through this stuff. And, alas, I have to live this stuff!

2013 was a tough year for me. I thought it was going to be my breakout year, and, instead, it turned out to be my breakthrough year.

I was teetering gleefully on the edge of a much bigger business. Things were going great in 2012. I had leaped off some ledges, and I was flying high.

You will hear me say that I attribute a large part of my success to making the decision to hire my first business Coach in 2009, and I have not been without one since. At the end of each year, I am in search for my business coach for the new year.

Getting on my soapbox about this for a moment – I have not been without a Coach since 2009, and I would not ever be. I would not hire a Coach who didn't have a Coach. If you are a Coach or wanting to be a Coach and your business is not doing well or not even getting off the ground, you need to hire a Coach. You cannot sell something you yourself do not believe has value. If you are not using it in your business and your life, you can't convey to others why they should.

Okay, back to my story…

I didn't know what I didn't know, so I came into 2013 with some skewed thinking and some off-track perceptions about what I most needed right then. I was seeing success up close and personal, and I had a big goal I wanted to achieve in this new year, and I went for it. I made some big mistakes, and I learned a lot.

What clouded my judgment and kept me from that next level of success was a story I was holding onto and allowing to have power over me, my life and my business. My husband and I had made a big lifestyle move, preparing to be empty nesters, and creating the life we wanted to live in this next stage of our journey together. Everything was going great. But something happened with the house we were living in before, and things stopped going the way we had planned.

We had a house, a much bigger house, and we had to keep paying for it and maintaining it, stuck in the past, while trying to move forward into this wonderful present we had created for ourselves. Everything in our current world was completely aligned and delivering us the life of our dreams, while we kept being pulled back into the past with this house. I got stressed, and angry, and I created a story about it which followed me into 2013.

"I can't hire the Coach I really need right now, because that house won't sell." "I can't join the program I really need, because the house won't sell." "I can't get that great office I have always wanted, because the house won't sell."

It held me back. I told the Universe the story, and, so, it was.

"Whatever you say is, IS."

I struggled all year long. I hired Coaches that were not the Coach that I needed and wanted. I put off making the best decisions for my business. I played it small. I played it safe. I played it wrong. And it started affecting my life. As the story grew bigger, it created more and more sorrow and pain for me.

Until I had finally had enough. And I had to drink my own medicine.

I had a lot of private clients in my coaching program and students coming into my Spiritual Business School. What was I telling them? What was I speaking to others at retreats and meetings, on telesummits and radio shows?

I allowed myself to stay stuck almost all year long, and then I had enough. That November, I pulled myself out of my story, and I looked at what I teach and what I believe. I did the hardest thing. I made a decision. I owned it 100%. I believed, and I took action. And that's when everything in my world and my business changed! Only then did the Universe conspire on my behalf.

I had to laugh. Of course. I knew it all along. And I could have done this earlier, but I chose to learn the lesson. I will say, it served me so well as I marched full speed ahead through the beginning of the next year. What I learned was invaluable. It had to be.

Within days, I got a free ticket to an event from the Coach I really wanted to hire. I knew this was the push I would need, so I made the trip happen.

I came home, and I took the next step. I hired the Coach. It was scary given my current circumstances. And here's what happened next...

Within 24 hours, I got a new client that paid me double what my deposit for the Coach was. And, after that, four more new clients showed up, enrolled in my private coaching program and paid me in full. The amount of money that came in that week covered the costs of this Coach for the entire year.

When I stepped up, the clients stepped up.

Then, an office space became available where I have been wanting an office for several years, and I took it...

... and then my house sold!

... and I got more new clients showing up, ready to get started and paying in full!

... and some extra money came in that we had been waiting on for 10 years!

What story are you telling the Universe right now about how it is that is not serving you?

I tell my clients and students all the time, you can't play the when/then game with the Universe. So many people have come to me over the years telling me when I have all this taken care of, when I have all this come in, when I have all this in line, then I will step out and live my Purpose, answer my calling, build my business, do what I am made to do.

The problem is, that will never work. I have never seen it work yet. And, believe me, I used to try it, too. All it created for me was a lot of pain and struggle and confusion. You are always asked to take the first step. Then the Universe will rush in to conspire on your behalf. All manner of things show up in response to assist you.

Notes:

Chapter Nine: How Is Your Confusion Currently Serving You?

Confusion. It's one of the things I most often see keeping people stuck. Whenever you get stuck in Confusion, the first thing you want to do is to remember your touchstone, your Vision. The clearer your Vision, the easier it is to make decisions and choices, because each choice you come to is an opportunity to make a decision that will either move you toward or away from your Vision.

Ask yourself, "What is my priority right now? What can I do right now to make this happen?"

Go back to your Vision, and then go back to the question, and that will help you get out of Confusion when you are faced with all these different pieces, remembering that everything moves you either away from or toward your Vision. Every day, you will have decisions. There will be choice points in every moment, and the more you are aware of this, you won't get stuck in it. You will keep moving forward. Keep doing this until it becomes easier, until it becomes more natural in a flow and habit.

At first, it's like training, like an Olympic athlete having to train. You're really having to rewire yourself physiologically, you're having to reset your mindset. You're having to reset the mode of whether you're responding or reacting. You're have to reset the way you interact with your environment and the people and the things in your environment. Know that this is a process.

Get very good at being willing to stop and make that change and make that shift. Keep revisiting your Vision. At first, when you wake up every morning, make it a habit, make it a part of your success plan, your personal success strategy, to bring that Vision to mind and recommit yourself to it and then move forward into your day.

That way, it's on top of your mind. You've programmed your subconscious to understand exactly what to be looking for, because you've said, "Here's what I want. Here's my big Vision." We have millions of bits of information that come into our sensory perception throughout every day, and you have a reticular activating system in your body that says, "Pay attention to this; don't pay attention to that."

A lot of time, when we're getting a lot of Confusion, we start asking questions, and questions are very good in the right energy. What we tend to do is get into a state of constriction, where we're almost folding in over ourselves and asking questions.

Sometimes, we're asking questions that aren't helping. "Why? Why is this always happening to me? Why can't I make it work? What's going on here? I don't know what to do." It brings constricting energy. It brings constriction of everything within us. You do not want to get into that space.

What you want to do is come into a state of expansion where you're asking open-ended questions. Again, when you're asking, "Why is this always happening to me?" The Universe will always answer any question, anything you send out, and those tend to have a lot of energy, a lot of feeling behind them. What you'll get is consistent evidence of why this is happening to you. What that's going to look like is more and more lessons, more and more of what you believe always happens to you, never happens to you, whatever it is.

When you ask, "Why is this always happening to me? Why can't I?," you're asking for feedback. The Universe is going to give it to you, and it's going to look like more of what you don't want.

So, when you stop and you get into a state of expansion, you want to ask questions that the Universe can bring you answers to. You want to say, "What is possible? What could be better? What could be more? How can I make an impact today? How can I make more money today? How can I be in a more loving relationship today?"

Whatever you are asking, the Universe is answering, so keeping yourself in a state of Confusion is always a choice. There is something you are refusing to see, or there is something you are refusing to respond to. It's there. Wherever there is a need and a desire, there is also the ability to fulfill it. Now.

When you are faced with Confusion, a couple of things are going on. The first thing you do is say, "Oh, this is Confusion." You can choose to stay in a confused state. I will tell you, if you're staying in a confused state for any length of time, you're choosing to do that, and it's serving you. Then, you need to go back and take honest inventory and figure out why you are needing to stay in this state.

When faced with Confusion, there is always something you can do to move out of Confusion.

One, your Purpose is not clear enough, and you are not attached enough to it. You haven't bought into it. You can't envision it enough. You're not fully there, or you don't fully believe it can happen. You don't have a strong enough "Why?"

Go back, at this point, to your Purpose, Vision and Why, and work on these things. Explore your vision. Explore your Mission. Explore your Dreams, and explore your Truth. Your Purpose is the fuel. The Confusion is the brakes.

Another thing that can be going on is that you have a conflict within you. You may not be aware of it. It's very likely you aren't. You are not in alignment in all levels of your awareness.

Parts of you are on board. Inside of you, you have all these different levels of awareness, and there are parts of you that are not buying into the Vision and are not going there, because they have determined some level of it not being safe or not being comfortable, or there's a belief that's getting in the way. These beliefs can be getting in the way and putting on the brakes.

The other thing that can be going on is that you don't know. You get into confusion, and you get overwhelmed. "I lack the skills. I lack the resources." In this case, determine what is going on and what you need to know to move forward. If this is the case, ask yourself, "Hey, what do I need to know?" "Do I really not know?" This is where you start chunking it down, if it feels really big.

Just start with, "What is one thing I need to know?" and take an action in that direction.

114

Be willing to take a look at yourself and see which of these things is going on. Take 100% responsibility to push through your Confusion. Recognize it as Resistance. Once you determine which of these things is going on, you need to sit down and say, "What do I need to do right now?" You know. By now, you know what you need to do next. And, then, you ask yourself this, and this is where the rubber meets the road, "Am I willing to do this?"

I cannot tell you how many people, and you will know this is true, how many people know exactly what they need to do next, and they're just not doing it. They keep saying, "I don't know what to do next," or, "I can't do what I need to do next." "I don't have the time." "I don't have the money." "I don't know where to start."

It's that simple. Because once you get honest with yourself, and you start asking yourself these questions and answering them, Boom! "What do I need to do next?" "I know this is what I need to do next." "Am I willing to do this, yes or no?" Yes? Okay, now you know what you need to do next! No? Okay, now you are being honest, and you really aren't confused at all.

And now you are getting Clarity, and that is the first step to move you forward in the direction of your dreams and desires to create a better life now!

If your answer here is "No," then it's time to go back to emotional mastery, energy management, intuitive development and taking honest inventory. These are all aspects of my programs.

Regardless, you keep working through it. You don't stop. If you're asking yourself questions, you take it to deeper and deeper levels. You don't get stuck in Confusion.

If it's too big, you chunk it down. You chunk it way down. You chunk it way, way down, and you seek help and guidance when you need it.

"I'm confused. I'm stuck." is an excuse. Confusion is a defense mechanism. It does not serve you. It creates a story, and allows you to live in that story, if you choose. It is a distraction, and it is ultimately avoidance.

Recognize it. Own it. Push through Resistance into Receptivity. Get started right now.

Lions and Tigers and Beliefs, Oh My!

Every day, in the work I do, I come across beliefs that have taken root in people and are keeping them from moving forward, creating what they desire, and maintaining their successes.

These beliefs are driving your bus, and yet, much of the time you are not even aware of them. At some point, they became a part of you. Now, they are holding you back.

Identifying and letting go of beliefs that no longer serve you is at the heart of transformation work, be it personal or spiritual.

It begins with a belief you have accepted, usually very early in your life, and over time it has become fact. Your subconscious uses this belief to navigate you through your daily life, and you are nudged to notice everything that is in line with and supports this belief. Thus, you get what you expect.

I have seen miracles occur as soon as a belief is loosened and dissolved and replaced with a more powerful and supportive belief. Reality is restructured. Life begins to be very different.

Affirmations were all the craze a few years ago. Positive thought. And yet, people continue to show up and tell me, "I am saying all these affirmations, and they are not working." That's because you can't fool the body. And the Universe does not listen to your words. It responds to your emotions – your energy in motion.

In order to transform a limiting belief into an empowering belief, you have to:

- Get in touch with the belief.
- Determine the strength of the belief.
- Connect with the feelings around the belief.
- Crack through the resistance the limiting belief is creating.
- Build a new belief.

Recently, I led my clients through an exercise to do just this. I recorded this class and now have made it available to you. Listen online or download it to go at
http://instantteleseminar.com/?eventid=28163235

I know how powerful and life-changing this work can be. It's a game-changer. Imagine doing this work with your own personal coach walking you through it step-by-step. Imagine working on your beliefs from many levels at one time – physically, energetically, mentally, emotionally and spiritually. Imagine shifting a belief that has a hold on you and beginning to create more good in your life.

Pick a belief, any belief, and get started bringing it to the surface, so you can deal with it head on. And pretty soon, "Toto, I've a feeling we're not in Kansas anymore!"

All it takes is a little courage.

Transformation is within your reach. As Dorothy says, "If I ever go looking for my heart's desire again, I won't look any further than my own back yard." It begins within, right in your own "back yard."

Chapter Ten: Moving Forward Might Not Get You There

You know, you can be moving forward and still not getting where you want to go.

I work with a lot of people who get stuck, frozen and paralyzed with inaction, and sometimes they stay that way for a long time. Suddenly, they have filled their time and their lives with distractions, excuses and obligations. They feel confused without realizing that confusion is a form of self-sabotage. If you wait for confusion to turn to clarity on its own, you will wait a very long time.

Lately, though, I have had some clients showing up who, by all appearances, are moving forward. They have created success in their lives in some areas, only to realize now that their success does not align with their core values, and that often they have forfeited what is important to them, their dreams and their heart's desires, in the process. Then something happens. Life changes. Suddenly, they find themselves facing a major life moment or anticipating one, and they come face to face with their utter dissatisfaction at the state of their lives.

But, hey, they are go-getters, action-takers, and they are used to digging in and making things happen. And so they plod on. Yet, inside nothing miraculous changes. They may receive awards and accolades, many of them receive pretty hefty paychecks, and they have nice things to show for it. When they look around, the things they want most are not present, and they can't figure out how to get them.

The solution lies in our energy, in our thoughts and beliefs and in the very actions we are taking and not taking. When we look at what we really want, the way to it at first isn't clear. We must unravel what appears on the surface and dive deeper.

Working with energy is amazing. We can literally change our world, and fast. I have women creating new lives for themselves in just 90 days. The secret is to begin to make these shifts and changes and create joy in your life now, and little by little, the energy of that grows, and things begin to show up in a different and better way, in a new way. The more joy you have, the better things get. And so on, and so on.

So, yes, it is possible to be moving forward and yet not be able to get where you are going.

We have a choice point in every moment, and every choice we make and action we take, moves us either towards or away from what we most desire. Nothing is neutral. This is one of the 9 Guiding Principles I use in my teachings and my work with my clients and students.

My Coach's Request To You: Look where you are going. Whatever is showing up for you now is going to continue to show up for you if you keep doing what you're doing. It may show up in different forms, but if you really pay attention, you will begin to see patterns and energies that are in play here.

Take some reflection and meditation time to revisit your core values. What do you want your life to look like? What is important to you?

If we first create the Vision, then we can create everything else to build and support the life we desire. And that will bring us Joy, which will bring us even more of the life we desire, which will bring us even more Joy.

If you have fallen out of the Cycle of fulfilled desires and Joy, YOU can create a better life now. You can make a decision to get moving in the direction of your dreams and desires. Think of steering a large ship or a jet airplane. Working with the energy and momentum that is being created and turning that around can be challenging at first, but once you reset your course, everything falls in line, and it gets easier and more effortless with every mile. And, the most important thing of all is, now you are moving forward in the right direction, and you will be able to get to where you are going.

Notes:

Chapter Eleven: Climb Out Of The Crab Bucket

"When people undermine your dreams, predict your doom, or criticize you, remember, they're telling you their story, not yours."

I love this story one of my coaches told me, and it has really stuck with me. In fact, I use it as an example for where people are stuck, because so many can identify with it. I observe this all the time with people in my community, and with my clients and students.

Have you ever watched crabs in a bucket, she asked me? The bucket does not have a top on it, and yet the crabs are not able to escape. If there is only one crab in the bucket, it can and will escape easily. However, when there are many crabs in the bucket, as soon as one crab tries to escape by climbing out, the other crabs will grab hold of it and pull it back down into the bucket to share the mutual fate of the rest of the group.

As you begin to get the urge for a fuller experience of life and a fuller expression of yourself, when you respond to the calling and make the choice to step onto this path, to take the first step of the journey, often you find there are those who are not there to support you. They want you to stay in the bucket. Some people are very invested in having you stay the same. It takes support and guidance to climb out of the bucket, to make a choice and commitment to yourself to be a Conscious Creator.

This is the perfect time to begin plugging into supportive and like-minded communities and getting connected with a coach or mentor.

Perhaps you've been very well socialized to live a "normal" life. Yet, something is calling to you to be more, do more, and have more. The standards being set in our world today often speak to the path of mediocrity; live by this set of rules, norms and expectations, and you will get by. This way of living limits your growth, the reaching of your highest potential, and the creation of your best life. It limits your greatness. Those who respond to the calling of their Higher Self toward all they desire discover something; they discover their authentic selves, make a choice to expand beyond existing, to evolve and excel. They take action to create a life they love, the life of their dreams.

As you move into higher consciousness, connecting with your Truth becomes a stronger call. When you are in alignment with your Truth and begin to spend more of your time and energy consciously creating, your life FLOWS! You begin to attract to you everything you need. Things begin to come together more easily and effortlessly. Call it synchronicity. Call it miracles.

Move out of pain and frustration, out of feeling trapped or stuck, out of a life that no longer serves you and feels like it no longer fits. Learn to use your energy to move into the life you desire, something that is more in alignment with living your truth.

Who are you showing up as? The crab in the bucket shaming others who go for their greatness while hiding behind your own "spirituality?" Or one of the crabs who has climbed out of the bucket and is finding your way through this Entrepreneurial Hero's Journey? www.ClimbOutOfTheCrabBucket.com

How To Get Your Dreams Out Of Your Head And Into The World

"It takes third-dimensional action to create third-dimensional results. It takes massive third-dimensional action to create massive third-dimensional results."

Act: Your next step is the one that most people get stuck at, and many do not move forward at this point, often for many, many years, sometimes for a lifetime. You must take new action to get new results. Learn to read the feedback, do your work in the physical third-dimensional world, and allow the Universal Energy to work with you and for you. Energy Healing works in the Fifth Dimension. The Fourth Dimension is where we work with our thoughts and feelings. When we stop here, we create a rich inner world that is not reflected in our outer world. We long to escape more and more into this world. Our physical world continues to deteriorate. At some point, we begin to lose the ability to create what we need to meet our basic needs. We are left longing for love, money, relationships, fulfilling work, a home that is our sanctuary, and other worldly things that continue to elude us.

Notes:

A Client Story: From Lawyer To Life Purpose

You have got to hear about this!

I had a call a few months ago that is one of those moments that makes living in your purpose worth it, no matter what.

I have a client who came to me a year ago. She was a lawyer earning six figures and feeling like she was not living her purpose, had gifts emerging that she wanted to express, and she was working in a toxic environment that was making her sick. But she was making really, really good money, and she was the primary breadwinner for her family, and she had children, and her husband's job was on shaky ground, and the house needed major repairs. And. And. And.

The first thing I did with her on our first call was to help her subconscious mind stop spinning and draining her energy. I asked her, tell me a date you absolutely will no longer tolerate living like this. She told me January 4, 2015. At the time, it felt very far off. We were at the end of 2013, just heading into 2014. But this helped a lot, because it kept her mind from asking her every day, how long are you going to stay here, when will this be over, how much more of this can you take?

Then we started to do the work.

We created a Vision of the life she wanted to live. We looked at what was showing up that she didn't want. We looked at what she already had that she did want.

I helped her start building the business of her dreams.

And her stuff came up. I mean, it really came up.

She didn't back down.

She worked on her oldest, most painful stuff that was holding her back. She peeled layer after layer of it away, and great and wonderful things emerged.

She faced her fears. She worked her way through anxiety attacks.

She kept building her business, and the blessings came as she began to Be and Do more and more in her purpose every day.

These are techniques I use with my clients a lot, especially the ones who come to me and want to leave the situations they are in and create new ones.

The more we did this work, the more Spirit intervened on her behalf. She learned to leave the how's to the Universe, and the Universe made connections, lined up opportunities and cleaned things up for her.

It's been an amazing journey to watch and an amazing journey to be a part of. We have both been blessed in the process.

When she first came to me, and she didn't believe what she desired was possible, wasn't certain that what she was being called to do was doable, I stood in a place and held space for her. I believed…

… because I had done it myself, and I knew.

Yesterday, she quit her job. She is owed paid time that she will receive money for but no longer have to show up in that place, and when it's all said and done, it will be January 4, 2015!

She is already creating income with her own Spiritual Business, and the moment she let go, new opportunities began to show up, all coming together to show her, you are supported, you are taken care of, you did the right thing. Bravo!

Someone, hand me a Kleenex! It was a moment to behold. In that moment, I trusted it all. Again.

The journey's not over yet. In fact, it's just beginning. I am talking about the journey where you create a Vision of the life you want to live and then create a business that supports and sustains it.

Come on, I tell her, I know the way. I've been doing this a little while. I'll hold space for you, and I'll hold your hand.

She and I will be continuing our journey together through 2015. She said, I still need you. I know. I haven't been without a Coach since 2009, and I wouldn't be.

I love working with people at this level, bringing all my gifts to the table to support and guide you through the inner work and the outer work.

I have made space in my calendar to work with 6 clients at this level in 2015. You need to be willing to show up. You need to be willing to stay in it for the long haul to get the results you want. You need to trust me and trust the process.

Come on. I know the way. I've been doing this a little while. I'll hold space for you, and I'll hold your hand.

A Letter Written To A Client

Client: Here Is What Is Holding Me Back.

Me: Here Is What To Do About It.

Hi, Dear Client,

I love this, and you are right on track. These are all beliefs, not Truth, and they will hold you back. I just busted through a belief of my own this week and had a big payday from it. So, I know it works.

"There is too much work to do to be ready for success." – I teach my clients and students to create success right away. Within as little as the first 30 days, they have clients or more clients and are making money or more money. You want to create right away a business that will support and sustain the life you want to live, and it's very doable. Yes, there is work to do, but that doen't mean it can't pay off from the beginning. I have run my business from the beginning being willing to be perfectly imperfect, and so I have consistently grown more clients and more money and a bigger and better business which led to a bigger and better life. You don't get ready for success. You create it right now today. You are in business now.

"I have to work hard, for free, before people will pay me." - I actually put a stop to this immediately with my clients and students. I have a formula for giving away for free for a short period of time, but with a clear strategy, and there still has to be an

energy exchange. You should actually not give away for free. The reason I am able to give so much away for "free" all the time and love doing it is because I have built it into the structure of my business, it's part of the system, and I am making plenty of money in my business. It's part of my business strategy, structure and system, and the free has purpose and pays off for me while it's serving my community.

"Nobody has money to pay a reasonable amount for my work." – This was a big one for me. My ideal client or target market doesn't have money to pay, and I bought into it, until enough Coaches making money and growing businesses like the one I wanted to have told me it's simply not true unless I believe it is. I bumped up against this one recently and made a big shift and had a big payday. People pay me really good money for what I do now, and those who can pay show up and pay me willingly, and they get results. This all comes down to you valuing yourself and your work and putting it out in the world in a strategic way.

"People don't respond to posts or emails." – Again, I have created a system and a structure, and people e-mail me all the time, respond to my e-mails, open my e-mails, and buy what I am offering. I have tons of engagement with my posts. It's strategic, using that word again. I now run my entire business off Facebook, and it works very well for me. You just have to understand how it will work for you and have a plan. Once I did that, my business grew to a full-time business bringing in consistent clients and income.

"It seems like people don't care about their personal success and happiness. The focus is only on debt, physical complaints, and just surviving their current state."– True in a way, and you won't change that. It's the human condition. Believe me, it broke my heart to discover it's the same even with "enlightened" people, often more so, which baffles me. We walk around saying we are here to make an impact and change the world, but then many won't invest in changing themselves or take the action to change themselves, and that would change the world. We say we believe in an Abundant, Infinite Universe, and yet so many are living in poverty and tolerating it, and living with illness and debt and toxic relationships, putting themselves in toxic environments every day. I know, it's a tough stance to take. I have been a helper and healer my whole life, and I used to want to "save" and "rescue" people, and it doesn't ever work. Something about those things is serving them, as it was serving me for many years, until I got real with myself, took honest inventory, and took my personal and spiritual growth and development seriously. That was the path I chose. We each get to choose.

People do care about their personal success and happiness, and they say they want it. More and better money, work, relationships and life. But people in general will not move in the direction of their pleasure. They wait to be motivated by their pain. They move only when they are in enough pain away from what causes them pain. This was a huge life-changer and game-changer for me, when I started learning to move always toward my pleasure, so now I don't wait to get into pain, and I don't bring that pain into my life. For years, I did. Again, I tested this for a long time, and I wanted to find different results. Even "enlightened" people on a personal and spiritual growth path will not necessarily invest in this journey, because they have bigger pains. Even though, this would help move them out of this situation and circumstance, they don't often take the risks. They don't buy. You have to learn to find out what they need right now, and you offer them that, and then you give them all of what you have to offer.

"My potential customers face the same challenges as me. (This isn't that 'bad'.)" – Yes, they do, and this is the path to the most success, especially financially, in building and growing your business. You are on a journey. You have something to teach people right now, and that's all you have to have right now. You have your story and your experience, and you step out and share that, and you attract a community to serve. As they grow, you grow, and you and your work evolve. I have been the most successful in branding myself, sharing my story, sharing my journey, and it has changed over the years – you know, because you have been following me for a long time – and I am willing to invest in myself and grow, and so I serve my community and my clients, and new ones show up in response to what I have learned that I can share with them. If you wait until some perceived time when you will be ready, you are missing the only opportunity that exists now, and you will not be any more ready later, and you will remain in struggle.

"So what stops me? Pain, lack of investment money with a tight budget, uncertainty a plan will or is working, uncertainty I CAN do this to the fullest degree desired, and I don't want to work two full time jobs, it's too much energy spent and not enough in return." - This one always gets me. I struggled with it

myself. When I invested in my first Coach, I had no idea how I could pay every month. I kept taking inspired action, and I stayed aligned with my Purpose, and I created the money every month. I have not been without a Coach since 2009, and I have invested in myself consistently since 2009. Recently, I knew I needed to invest at a much higher level for 2014. So what would that require of me? I had to create the money. I didn't have any of it. I started taking consistent inspired action. I stayed with it, and I created the money, more than I needed in one hour one day because of aligned action I kept taking leading up to it. I wrote down my goals on my calendar, and I reached them. I had many Coaches tell me this is the way it works.

The Universe only responds to true need, yet people seem to be waiting until they have a pile of extra money laying around, and then they will invest in themselves. It doesn't usually work that way. So why wait for that? Every time I have invested in myself, once I made the commitment and had true need, the money showed up. It often showed up as opportunity that I had to step into. I am asking to be more, do more and have more, so more is going to be required of me. And it often wasn't comfortable or logical or reasonable or clear on how I could do it. But I did it anyway. I did it this week. I created the money for what I needed to move me forward. I didn't give up. I had a hissy fit a few weeks ago. I got pissed. I got irritated. I felt sorry for myself. But I didn't give up. And I kept following the system I know works, and I got coaching and support, and I created exactly what I needed, and more. And it came out of nowhere from someone I had not known that found me and wanted what I had to offer, because I was still out there offering it. It found me. Do you hear that? You have to do your part, and then the Universe is the best networker and will make the match.

"The picture of my current lifestyle is feeling like a different, lower vibration, boring, in comparison to what I want which is full of light, happiness, flow, helping others and feeling supported, no struggle." – I get it. I will no longer tolerate living in low vibration. I know when I get in it, and I change it. I use my tools. I use my support. You cannot create and attract that which you want unless you are being it, doing it and having it. I start with my clients having them add those things into their lives in the smallest way, consistently. And there is mindset work to be done. As you are matching up with it and attracting it in, it grows, and you receive more and more. You cannot create what you desire from a low vibrational state. The easiest state from which to manifest is Joy. Whatever you have highest desire for, you most often have highest resistance with, and that is why you need support and a plan, and you need to live it, not just do it sometimes. You create a new way of living and being until it becomes the way you are.

The other piece, you have to do the work to heal your money "stuff." I did a lot of it. I hired a Coach for six months to help me do it, and I continue to get Coaching around this issue. It's a big one, especially for Spiritual people. Do you see all the time on Facebook, people talking about how those rich people should be giving more and doing more and how rich people are evil or bad or greedy. They will never become what they despise, hate, judge. They just won't. Those are mindset that sabotage you and don't serve you, and unfortunately those in power and in the media and even in Hollywood perpetuate those stereotypes, because that keeps you out of your power and easier to control. It's all stories. You have powerful money stories that are keeping you right where you are. I had a lot of money "stuff."

That's why I'm so passionate now about healing that in my Community. Some will go in that direction. Others will stay where they are, in poverty, and it's very sad, but I will no longer try to convince, save or rescue them. I will live my life by example. The people I now surround myself with have helped me build new beliefs. They are Spiritual, Intuitive, Creative Healers and Helpers with thriving work they are doing in the world, and they are giving back to the world in very big ways. How about we create more of that? First, these people need to heal their money "stuff" and start taking action aligned with their desires and stay with it. There are a lot of beliefs that need shifting and actions that need taking. This is nothing new. It's in all the Spiritual and Success texts and teachings we have in the world.

"I feel it's 'all or nothing.' Little efforts don't get me very far, and so I think that is why I start and stop projects." – It feels that way at first. Yet, I have found baby steps, consistently, every day, in alignment with your desires, creates profound changes. It starts building exponentially. Every time you stop and start that energy, you have to essentially start over. You are sending a message to the Universe that you are not committed and that you do not have a true need, so the Universe says, okay, let me know when you have a true need and you are ready. I'm here. My business has grown to where it is today, and so my life has also grown, by not stopping and taking actions. Some days, I don't feel like it, so I start with

the smallest action, I am going to get dressed and go to that lunch, or just send one e-mail or touch base with someone, do something, and then the energy starts working for me, and I either continue on or give myself some time off to do other things. I take aligned inspired action every day, no matter what, and I work on my "stuff" when it comes up no matter what. I am never without support and guidance.

If all that feels very hard or overwhelming, I will tell you the reason I can speak so boldly now is not only because I do it, so I walk my talk with this, and I would never ask you to do anything that I do not do, but also because I have served enough clients now that do these things, too, and they have great results and outcomes. And I have more than enough people who have helped me build new beliefs about all this.

"I have a lot of creative ideas, and I know I can solve many issues and find solutions, but I don't see how I can speed up MY self development, because it is tied to this. Working for a company is easier because I don't feel it is me determining if my efforts are good enough, as the final say." - This is something big to look at for you. It sounds like a big piece right now with a lot of things tied into it. You want to be applying Universal Principles and all these things I am talking about immediately and consistently. It's not just something you do, it's a way of living and being, and you learn to do it more and more as you do it and grow. I don't ask most of my clients to step out of their jobs or let of their security. Only those who say that is their intention, I support and guide them in that. Clients working with energetic principles and doing the energetic work first are able to much more easily and

naturally come out of those things they don't love that no longer serve them and are able to attract better things in the process.

If you have a desire for something, there is a way, right now. It is going to take risks and work, but it doesn't have to be a negative experience. I get my clients out in the world using their gifts and being paid for that right away. It's the way to create money for your personal and spiritual growth journey, to have the life you want to have, and it's the way to support and sustain yourself in living the life you want to live.

Notes:

Chapter Twelve: Consistency Equals Success

Consistency is absolutely one of the key success strategies to apply to any area of your life where you are seeking positive change.

It is also something I resisted for a very long time. I am a spontaneous Soul. I thrive in environments that offer variety. I love the unexpected. I am a crisis and trauma specialist and worked in that field for many years. I am hard-wired that way. What I didn't like was routine, structure, sameness of any kind.

And then I applied the value of Consistency to a business that was perplexing me and frustrating me, and voila! The magic ingredient.

You can't deny it; without consistency, you will eventually falter in even your best efforts.

Consistency equals success. Ask any business building or growth and development specialist in the industry.

I found quite a few quotes when I "Googled" the subject. And what I came across was very interesting. There is a place where consistency serves you and a place where consistency keeps you stuck.

What works for me is to apply consistency to my business and my life in a very purposeful way while remaining fluid and flexible. When I am clear on what is important and what is not, I am able to make beneficial decisions in every moment.

For instance, Benjamin Disraeli said, "The secret of success is consistency of purpose."

You want to be really clear on your purpose for doing anything. Purpose is a common thread that runs through the tapestry of your life, holding it all together in a meaningful way.

If you are serving clients or customers, you want to be consistent in your communication with them and your service to them.

If you are dissatisfied with any area of your life, look closely at what you are consistently doing and not doing. This will tell you what is keeping you from having what you want.

You may have heard the quote, "It takes twenty years to become an overnight success." Eddie Cantor said it, and there is much truth in this.

Aristotle said, "We are what we repeatedly do. Excellence, then, is not an act, but a habit," and it still holds true today.

Cultivating persistence and establishing consistency will put you on track for the personal success you desire.

Before You Get Into The Daily Doing

Before you get into the daily doing that is required, do some inner work around clarity of your purpose. What are you here to do? What nudges at you? What drives you? What lights you up?

Now envision what you want your life to look like, what you want each day to look like, down to the details, and really anchor your purpose into that.

This is where you want to begin. What kind of life are you wanting to create for yourself? What is your purpose and how can you express it in a way that supports you in living this life that you desire and deserve?

And now I want you to connect with your WHY. This is what helps you be persistent and consistent no matter what. Until I had a big enough WHY and really was connected to it, I gave up and I gave in more than I kept going. Now, nothing throws me off track for very long. I do not get distracted, and I do not get derailed.

My Coach's Request To You: Explore these things now. VISION. PURPOSE. WHY. Really spend time with them. Then take honest inventory of what needs to be consistently happening and whether it is or isn't. Set some new intentions. Make a decision about something you are going to consistently do for the next 30 days.

See what happens!

Notes:

In Closing, I Offer You This: Are you merely interested or committed?

"There's a difference between interest and commitment. When you're interested in doing something, you do it only when circumstances permit. When you're committed to something, you accept no excuses, only results." — Art Turock

I still remember the day, sitting in San Diego in a conference aimed at getting me in touch with and connected to my big mission and my big life, and the woman on stage, looking right at me, asked, *"Are you merely interested or committed?"*

Wow! What a question. That one not only spoke to me; it reached out and grabbed me by the shoulders and shook me a little. Up until that moment, I had been dabbling, playing in the possibilities, dreaming about all the things I could do and would do. I had big intentions. And yet, I was dancing around the edges, dipping my toe in, surveying the surface, without diving in.

She called me to action that day, and nothing has ever been the same since. Everything I had learned and experienced up to that moment had prepared me to step into the fullness of it. All I had to do was show up, just as I was.

Randy Pausch, who is well-known for his speech *The Last Lecture, said,* "The brick walls are there for a reason. The brick walls are not there to keep us out; the brick walls are there to give us a chance to show how badly we want something. The brick walls are there to stop the people who don't want it badly enough. They are there to stop the *other* people!"

It's when you come to that place, your own brick wall, that you make a choice to either commit or retreat. You are always either moving towards or away from your goal, your vision, your mission, your truth. In that moment lies the opportunity to say, "I am doing this!," to face what is in your way, open up to the next step and move forward, doing what is necessary to create the future you are meant to be living now.

When you retreat, nothing happens. At first. But when you have a big vision, a mission calling to you, a purpose for being here on this planet that you are not expressing, and dreams for something better, it will eat away at you slowly. You will become more and more disconnected from your truth, from who you really are, and from your Source that feeds and supports you into your greatness.

I lived in this desert for a long time. Many years. I wandered in a wilderness of my own making. I cried out. I got stuck. I lost touch with myself, forgot my greatness. I found a million reasons why I could not, would not, should not pursue my purpose on this planet right then. I made promises to myself that I did not keep. It ate me alive from the inside out.

Something very important is always hiding just behind your resistance to making a commitment to yourself to step into who you are and take that out into the world. It's both the prison and the key to your freedom. Your choice in every moment defines it.

The moment you commit to yourself and to that greater something, everything changes. Your perspective changes. Instead of making excuses, you seek results.

It is said that, "Until one is committed, there is hesitancy, the chance to draw back, always ineffectiveness. Concerning all acts of initiative (and creation), there is one elementary truth, the ignorance of which kills countless ideas and splendid plans: that the moment one definitely commits oneself, then Providence moves, too. All sorts of things occur to help one that would never otherwise have occurred. A whole stream of events issues from the decision, raising in one's favor all manner of unforeseen incidents and meetings and material assistance, which no man could have dreamed would have come his way." -- J. W. von Goethe

This is precisely where the magic happens!

You must sound the call, engage first, and set in motion all that is ready to rush in to be a part of your creation and your bigger life, once you are ready for it.

I have had a lot of clients come to me playing the when/then game. They give me a list of what they want and tell me they will do everything I recommend to them if I can guarantee they will get what they want from doing it. At the same time, they tell their Trusted Source, "When you provide me with all of this, then I will answer the call."

That's not how it works. We came here for the experience. A perfect plan does not pre-exist; it becomes as we grow and evolve. It's an organic process, and it's miraculous.

Do you want it badly enough?

I see a lot of desire out there, and it's escalating for many people. What stops people is the moment they need to commit to themselves to take specific consistent action.

I often find that the higher desire someone has for something that is really important to them, the higher resistance they encounter. This is the opportunity to dive in and create astounding transformation. And it's scary as hell getting started. What it always is, I am here to tell you, it is worth it. Beyond measure.

You have a future that you are meant to live, and it's been calling to you. Where there is desire, there is always the way. You are meant to be living this life now. So, what's holding you back?

I can look back now over all the years that I knew what I wanted and who I wanted to show up in the world as, and I didn't do anything about it. I had tons of excuses, and I created a lot of busyness and distraction in my world. I did a lot to numb those cravings for more, and I promised myself that some day – SOME DAY – I would make a move. Just not today, I'm not ready, I'm not prepared, just don't ask me to do anything about it today.

You will come to moments like these in your own life, facing the pain of staying the same and the fear of creating change, and every time you make a choice to either commit or retreat. You are always, ALWAYS, either moving towards or away from your goal, your vision, your mission, your truth and the life of your dreams. There is an energy to it. In every one of these moments lies the opportunity to say, "I am doing this!," to face what is in your way, open up to the next step and move forward, doing what is necessary to create the future you are meant to be living now.

Something very important is always hiding behind your resistance, behind your excuses and your fears and doubts, that keep you from making a commitment to yourself to step into who you are and take that out into the world. It's both the prison and the key to your freedom. Your choice in every moment defines it.

Right now is one of those moments. As you read this, something is being activated inside of you, and you have a choice.

If you are ready to truly change the way you show up in your life and in your work, ready to experience a new way of being in your career, in relationships, with money, if you find yourself in just this place, then I challenge you to make a renewed commitment to yourself and take action now, today. Do something, from taking the tiniest baby step to the greatest leap, to get moving towards all that you want.

You are meant to be living this life now.

Know this: "The moment you commit and quit holding back, all sorts of unforeseen incidents, meetings and material assistance, will rise up to help you. The simple act of commitment is a powerful magnet for help." — Napoleon Hill

A Note About Risk-Taking

You may be really ready for a risk even after never having taken them; it can be such a liberating experience that yields magical results. I have been there and done it at a time when I disliked change and was very adverse to risk-taking. My life since then has been absolutely worth it, my journey exciting and yielding out-of-this world results. It takes a "new" mindset and tremendous support. It takes preparation the way you would prepare for any journey. When the timing is right, you will feel it and know it. When nothing will stop you and you know you can't not do this thing, then you are ready. That is the exact time to take the big risks and let the Universe rush in to support you.

A Reflective Exercise:

So, Just How Do I Get Started: Make A Decision to M.O.V.E.

"At any moment, the decision you make can change the course of your life forever." – Anthony Robbins

Make A Decision. Then Take Inspired Action that aligns with that decision. The number one thing that keeps people from realizing what they are trying to manifest is that they stop right at the crucial point of taking aligned action. They stop. Get stuck. Freeze. Feel paralyzed. Confused. Overwhelmed. All of this is Resistance. It means you are ready for a breakthrough. You have to take a new energetic stance and take new action that sends the message that things are changing. And they will. You have to make the first move to set things in motion.

Go into your heart space and know that you are going to create something wonderful for yourself today, right now. You are giving yourself a precious gift. You are showing up. Take a moment to recognize that everything in this moment is exactly as it should be. Remind yourself of all that you are grateful for. Then expand your desire for more and better. Focus on what you already have, and then focus on what you want. I desire. I can have. I do have. I know I already have. I believe I will have this.

Identify something that you would like to create.

Take a moment to focus on what that is. Just one thing. It is often beneficial to first choose something that you do not have a great amount of resistance to. You can bring this into your life more easily and build belief in yourself and this process.

As you focus on what it is that you desire and that you are committing to creating, notice what feelings arise within you. Be aware of your feelings, and be aware of any sensations in your body.

The first thoughts and feelings you have are often your greatest clues to core issues that are getting in the way, keeping you stuck and unfulfilled. This is your subconscious showing up briefly to give you the first glimpse of the underlying resistance. It usually comes in right on the heels of the desire, very fast. Catch it when it shows up, and then make note of it. Sit with your desire for a few minutes and notice all the sensations you experience, and allow them to move through your body and your mind.

Now, are you ready to Make A Decision to put the energy toward creating this thing you have identified and attracting it into your life?

Hold it dearly in your space, and get excited. Anticipate its arrival and you having it. Allow any discordant thoughts or feelings to come and go, acknowledging them and, for now, not giving energy to them.

For the next 21 days, you are going to focus on this thing, this desire, and know that it is yours. At first, it will require mindfulness and purposeful attention, and then it will begin to show up more often without as much effort ot bring it into awareness.

We are most open to our creative energy without resistance immediately upon waking, before our feet hit the floor, and just before falling asleep. This is the best time to focus on our desire and the knowing. This is the most optimal time to bring forth into our conscious awareness how we will feel when we have it.

Realize that the thoughts and feelings you hold in your consciousness just before falling asleep get powerfully imprinted, and messages are sent to your subconscious mind that act as a magnet to attract the match of that to you. Realize that the energy you begin your day with will shape the day you will have. Experiment with this, and see for yourself.

Check in with yourself as you hold the image of your desire. Is your heart on board? Is your mind on board? Is your body on board?

M = Make A Decision. The first step in my M.O.V.E. process.

It all starts with this.

Now, Get To It!

Know Where You Want To Be: You have been experiencing contrast. Every day you bump up against things that excite you and light you up and things that make you upset, irritated or angry. These are perfect opportunities to start talking to the Universe. Yes, I like this, I love this, give me more and more of it. I don't like this so much. I choose to focus on those other things I really, really want, and not give this any more attention. I don't want or need any more of it. When you are getting especially negatively charged by something, recognize it for the transformational tool it is. Pay attention! In this way, you begin to anchor at every level of your being where you want to be.

Always Move Toward, Never Away From: Now that you are beginning to create more awareness about what you want and where you are going, realize that there exists a choice point in every moment. Nothing is ever static. You are always – ALWAYS – moving either toward or away from what you want. Notice when you are moving closer to your dreams and desires and when you are doing things that move you away from them. Your feeling guidance system will let you know, so use it. You will begin to become more and more aware of what isn't serving you, and you will see that moving toward where you want to be will be easier once you start letting go of what no longer serves you.

Choose Mentors, Coaches and Teachers Who Are Where You Want To Be: You don't have to do this alone. My own coaches, teachers, mentors, healers and spiritual advisors have been invaluable to me throughout my personal journey and especially once I started building my business. Find those people who have what you want to have, who are doing what you want to do and are where you want to be, and start learning from them. Most people offer free resources you can get started with until you decide how you would like to invest in yourself and what is best for you. Surround yourself with inspirational and motivational material. I always have recordings available on my iPhone when I am traveling, driving in my car, or waiting somewhere. I have books that will educate and inform me and help me see things in new ways that are loaded onto my iPad.

Want More Support and Guidance?

Thank you for taking this Journey with me. It is my hope that you will integrate this information into your daily experience in every area of your life so that it becomes not just something that you do but a way of living and a way of being. I offer you a way of living that is powerful in its practicality and spiritually rich at the same time.

The principles are timeless, and they are absolute. We are operating within Laws of the Universe. The process itself is not always easy for us, and that is why I have Coaches, Teachers, Mentors and Guides to help me in my journey. I encourage and urge you to take a look at where you are and where you want to go this year, what you desire and what you want to create, and then consider one of the key principles of success, which is to work with your own personal Coach. Let me know how I can best serve you. www.michellebarr.com/contact

Notes:

My Gift To You: My 21-Day Email Course

It's Time to M.O.V.E. Forward Into A Better Life!

It is widely-known that it takes 21 days to create a new habit. To create inner change that is then reflected in your outer world, it takes working 21 days at all levels; physically, mentally, emotionally and spiritually.

It is important when we are creating a new habit to focus on the Be, Do, Have model.

Identify something that you would like to create and then commit to one new habit or way of being that you are going to integrate into your daily life for the next 21 days.

We must experience the Beingness of a person who is doing what we want to do and has what we want to have first. Then we must do what that person does which will move us into having what that person has.

During this process we are working on the brain and nervous system to create new responses and to eradicate old patterns of reacting. Brain circuits can create new neural net pathways only after they have been bombarded for 21 days in a row. Our brain does not accept new data to initiate a change of habit readily; this only happens after 21 days of repetition without missing a single day.

Can you do that? Are you merely interested or committed?

Make a decision to create a change in your mindset over the next 21 days, which will then be reflected back to you from your outer world, bringing you more of what you want and less and less of what you don't want.

If you do this consistently for the next 21 days, by the fourth week it will actually be more difficult for you not to engage in the new behavior than it would be to continue doing it.

You can choose a physical habit or a way of perceiving something.

If you really want to amp up your efforts, it has been shown that working on this at the same time of day every day during the 21 days is even more effective in helping you establish the new way of being.

Your new practice can also be better established by engaging as many of the senses as possible. Create an experience for yourself that includes certain smells, certain objects, clothing, music, occupying the same location, or assuming the same posture. Also, utilize your imagination. The more senses you can involve in creating the new habit the more likely it is to become ingrained in the neural pathways.

Reflect on this, and if you are ready to M.O.V.E., begin my 21-Day Email Course Now: *How To Get In Motion In Your Business And Your Life!* Get started at www.IntuitiveSuccessCoach.com

Who Is Michelle Barr?

Michelle Barr is an Entrepreneur, wife, mother and community connector who loves to inspire and motivate people to turn their life's calling into a profitable, freedom-based business and to create a life and a business they love.

As a full-time Coach, Speaker, Teacher, Author and Radio Show Host, Michelle serves as a Conscious Business Expert, Intuitive Strategist, and Mindset Mentor. Michelle serves her clients through her private and group coaching programs and products.

She is the Creator and Founder of Spiritual Business School and the Intuitive Women Entrepreneurs Network – A Global Initiative. A Kindred Community.

When Michelle first set out to follow her life's calling, she took several traditional paths that did not totally fulfill her or allow her to do her best work. So, she set out to create a business of her own. Her first business was started in her local community, and it quickly became a very expensive hobby, which created financial disaster for her and her family. Not willing to stop at this point, Michelle hired her first Business Coach and went on to create first a full-time local business and then a full-time thriving online global business.

Michelle created a Vision of the life she wanted to live and then created a business that supports and sustains that.

And now this is exactly what she loves to do for others!

Michelle has a bachelor's degree in Advertising, a master's degree in Counseling, and a seminary degree and ordination. She created her business by combining all of who she is and bringing the Counselor, Chaplain and Coach together to serve her clients and their Whole lives.

www.MichelleBarr.com

www.ingramcontent.com/pod-product-compliance
Lightning Source LLC
Chambersburg PA
CBHW060034210326
41520CB00009B/1119